S. Hrg. 113–420

CRISIS IN EGYPT

HEARING

BEFORE THE

COMMITTEE ON FOREIGN RELATIONS UNITED STATES SENATE

ONE HUNDRED THIRTEENTH CONGRESS

FIRST SESSION

JULY 25, 2013

Printed for the use of the Committee on Foreign Relations

Available via the World Wide Web: http://www.gpo.gov/fdsys/

U.S. GOVERNMENT PRINTING OFFICE

90–798 PDF   WASHINGTON : 2014

For sale by the Superintendent of Documents, U.S. Government Printing Office
Internet: bookstore.gpo.gov   Phone: toll free (866) 512–1800; DC area (202) 512–1800
Fax: (202) 512–2104   Mail: Stop IDCC, Washington, DC 20402–0001

COMMITTEE ON FOREIGN RELATIONS

(II)

CONTENTS

CRISIS IN EGYPT

THURSDAY, JULY 25, 2013

U.S. SENATE,
COMMITTEE ON FOREIGN RELATIONS,
Washington, DC.

The committee met, pursuant to notice, at 10:34 a.m., in room SD–419, Dirksen Senate Office Building, Hon. Robert Menendez (chairman of the committee) presiding.

Present: Senators Menendez, Boxer, Cardin, Shaheen, Murphy, Kaine, Markey, Corker, Rubio, Johnson, Flake, McCain, and Paul.

OPENING STATEMENT OF HON. ROBERT MENENDEZ, U.S. SENATOR FROM NEW JERSEY

The CHAIRMAN. This hearing of the Senate Foreign Relations Committee will come to order.

Thank you for joining us today for a timely hearing on the unfolding circumstances in Egypt.

I want to thank Ambassador Dennis Ross and Dr. Michele Dunne and Ambassador Daniel Kurtzer for being here today. We look forward to their perspective on the situation in Egypt and its ramifications for the region and for the United States.

The situation in Egypt has tremendous implications for the region and for the United States. Our response and our policy must be carefully calibrated to press for the Democratic reforms that have been demanded by the Egyptian people and at the same time support United States national security interests in the region.

These two goals are, in my view, not at odds with one another, but do require a complex policy response that allows us to advocate for much-needed democratic reforms, while also ensuring our own security needs.

At the end of the day, our policy and our laws must be nuanced enough to allow for a response that reflects our interests. And it is my view that terminating United States assistance at this time could provoke a further crisis in Egypt that would not be to our benefit.

Having said that, the future of our relationship with Egypt to a greater extent will be determined by our actions in the coming weeks, whether we will have a stable and willing partner on crucial matters of security, combating terrorism, trafficking of weapons and people into the Sinai, support for peace in the Middle East is up to us both.

Alternatively, we can stand aside during this crisis and just hope for the best. While our choices are difficult, at this time, in my view, abandoning Egypt would be a particularly poor policy choice.

But whatever policy we ultimately choose during this period of upheaval in Egypt, it is critical that all parties exercise restraint, that protests remain peaceful, and that violence is rejected.

The interim government should take those concerns to heart and, above all, ensure that the restoration of democracy be as transparent and inclusive as possible.

Steps that exacerbate the divide in Egyptian society, including the use of force against protesters, and arrests and harassment of pro-Morsi and of Muslim Brotherhood leaders serve only to deepen the chasm and forestall reconciliation.

The only way forward to a pluralistic, vibrant, and stable democracy lies in the inclusion of all political parties and groups.

Let me be clear, our support is not unconditional and unending. At the end of the day, Egyptian leaders and the Egyptian military must show that they are committed to an inclusive political process, credible democratic elections, and democratic governance that protects the rights of religious minorities and women.

On that subject, I am deeply concerned about the treatment of Coptic Christians, women, and Syrian refugees in a destabilized Egypt. The military and police forces must assure the safety of Egypt's minority groups, which means preventing the beating and killing of Christians and sexual assaults on women.

I am also disturbed by reports of Egypt turning its back on refugees fleeing the ever-worsening conflict in Syria. Egypt's military and interim government should provide safe haven for innocent civilians fleeing the brutality of the Assad regime.

I also hope that Egypt's security forces will be vigilant in the increasingly violent Sinai, where innocent Egyptians have been killed and terrorist groups have launched attacks against Israel.

Finally, Egypt's Government must quickly overturn the recent convictions of 43 NGO workers. Those sentences were a travesty of justice and must not stand. Their work to support the emergence of a strong pluralistic democracy is needed now more than ever.

I am hopeful that our panelists will leave us with a better understanding of the situation, the prospects for a peaceful, democratic resolution, and the choices that lie before us.

And with that, let me recognize our ranking member, Senator Corker.

STATEMENT OF HON. BOB CORKER, U.S. SENATOR FROM TENNESSEE

Senator CORKER. Thank you, Mr. Chairman. And I, too, want to welcome our witnesses. And given the dramatic changes that have occurred in Egypt since Mubarak's ouster over the last 2 years, I think it is critical that we take a look, take time to discuss our relationship.

I think sometimes we forget that we have critical national security interests in Egypt. It is the most populous country in the Middle East, a strategic ally, the recipient of more than $1 billion in U.S. taxpayer money, provides U.S. military vessels preferred access to the Suez Canal, and our two countries cooperative on counterterrorism.

So obviously, our policy right now is in a bit of a quandary. We are trying to decide how we move ahead with Egypt, how the issue of the coup affects, whether it was or was not, how it affects our policies going forward.

So I really do appreciate the witnesses coming in, giving us time to think with you as to how we move ahead with our policy, knowing the quandaries that we face in this relationship, but at the same time understanding the importance of Egypt as a strategic ally and, candidly, a very important entity in the region that we want to see stability prevail in.

So, Mr. Chairman, I thank you for having this hearing.

I thank you as witnesses, and I look forward to your testimony.

The CHAIRMAN. Thank you, Senator Corker.

With that, let me turn to our witnesses.

I am pleased to introduce Ambassador Dennis Ross, whose reputation and experience as a diplomat, Presidential advisor, and author made him one of the Nation's most respected foreign-policy minds on both sides of the aisle.

So welcome, Ambassador, back to the committee.

We also have with us Dr. Michele Dunne, vice president for the Atlantic Council and director of the Rafik Hariri Center for the Middle East. Dr. Dunne has served on the National Security Council staff in policy and planning, and the Bureau of Intelligence and Research at the State Department and as a diplomat in Cairo and Jerusalem.

Ambassador Daniel Kurtzer, now the S. Daniel Abraham Professor in Middle Eastern Policy Studies at the Woodrow Wilson School at Princeton, a great institution of the State of New Jersey and the Nation, served in the Foreign Service for almost three decades, and retired in 2005 with the rank of Career Minister and has been Ambassador in both Israel and Egypt.

Thank you all for being here. Your full statements will be entered into the record without objection. We ask you to summarize your statements in about 5 minutes or so, so that we can have a dialogue with you.

And with that, Ambassador Ross, if you will start.

STATEMENT OF HON. DENNIS ROSS, COUNSELOR, THE WASHINGTON INSTITUTE FOR NEAR EAST POLICY, WASHINGTON, DC

Ambassador ROSS. Thank you, Mr. Chairman. It is good to be here again.

The last time I was here, I was here to talk about Syria and the civil war there. And there is no question that both our morals and our strategic interests are engaged there. I would say when we talk about Egypt, though, the response is very different, the stakes are also very high, and our values and our interests are engaged there as well.

I find myself very much in agreement with what you were saying in your statement. When we look at Egypt, we know that Egypt is perhaps the most important Arab country. It has always been one that affects the rest of the region. Politically, culturally, it has been a trendsetter.

When we looked that the events of the Arab Awakening, they may well have begun in Tunisia, but it was the events in Tahrir Square that captured the imagination of the region and the world.

And I think once again, we are looking at events on the Egyptian street that are capturing everyone's attention. And it is a very unsettling situation, to say the least.

At a minimum, we have seen an elected leader removed. But I think when we look at this elected leader who was removed, we also have to understand that the intervention by the military was an intervention that was very much backed by a very large segment of the Egyptian population.

A critical mass of Egyptians feel that this leadership under President Morsi and the Muslim Brotherhood was a leadership that was not only not addressing Egypt's problems, it was more concerned with control than it was with governance. And while one can dispute the actual numbers that were on the petitions, and one can question how many people may have been on the street, there is no question that a very significant percentage of Egyptians reacted. And in many ways, one could describe what took place on June 30 and the events afterward as a popular uprising.

And the military used that popular uprising to remove President Morsi, but the reality is that today there is a good deal of support for what the military has done.

There are those within Egypt, there are those within the rest of the region, who would view what has taken place in Egypt as a course correction. And that helps to explain why you look at the Saudis and the Emirates and the Kuwaitis having pledged 12 billion dollars' worth of assistance, and obviously already beginning to act on that.

So there is one narrative that describes this very much as a kind of course correction of popular uprising. And there is obviously a different narrative. And that different narrative comes from the Muslim Brotherhood and the backers of President Morsi, who see what was a legitimately elected government replaced in what they see as an illegitimate way. And they have made it very clear that they demand the reinstatement of President Morsi. And they make it clear that they will not allow things to remain as they are, and they will continue to try to disrupt life within Egypt unless he is reinstated.

We have what can only be described as a depolarization within Egypt today. And while there may be rumors that there are efforts to mediate the differences, it is very difficult to see how those differences, at this point, are likely to be mediated.

I think that we are bound to see this polarization continue for some time. It is going to confront us, I think, with difficult dilemmas. I think we can look at the new interim government, which has many figures on it who are credible. For sure we look at Beblawi and a number of others. They are certainly very credible figures. But I think, at the same time, we have to recognize that the arbiter of events today are the military.

The first Deputy Prime Minister is General El-Sisi. You look at the speech he made yesterday in terms of calling on Egyptians to come out and support their efforts against terrorism, which is really another way of talking about their efforts against the Muslim Brotherhood, we are in for what is going to be, I think, a prolonged period of instability.

And we have big stakes in Egypt, as you were describing, so I think the real question for us becomes, what do we do now? And it is not as simple. Obviously, it is not a simple answer.

There are those who say that the right answer is for us to cut off assistance. I am not one of those. It is not because I do not understand the rationale behind doing that. It is not that I do not understand the arguments that are made. The notion that it was a coup, that we have laws, that we have principles, that we have to be credible to our principles, I take all this very seriously.

But I also take seriously the reality that the military's actions were supported by a significant percentage of the Egyptian population. And I also take seriously the need for us to maintain influence in the current situation.

I am afraid that if we were to cut off our assistance at this point, the effect of that would be that we would lose the link we have with the military. But we would also find a backlash among the Egyptian public.

The Egyptian public would look at this as an American effort. A critical mass of the Egyptian public would look at this as an American effort to dictate to them against the popular will. They would not take seriously our calls or statements that this is simply our law and these are our principles.

We would also find it would not have much resonance in the rest of the region. Most of the rest of the region, I think, is preoccupied with what is going on in Syria, and they do not see us there acting on the basis of our principles.

We would also see, I think, the Saudis and the Emirates and others very quick to fill in and take the place of our assistance beyond what they have already done.

And so I am concerned that basically the net effect of this would be that we would not have influence at a time when it is very much in our interest to try to affect what is going to happen.

I would not overstate the degree of our leverage, but I think it is critical for us to be prepared to use the leverage that we have.

And the military clearly wants us to maintain the relationship, for practical reasons. They also want it for symbolic reasons, because if we cut off assistance, it basically reinforces the narrative that the Muslim Brotherhood has put out there, and it will make it more difficult for the interim government, for the military, to get assistance from outside the region.

So the key for me is to use our leverage—not to be reluctant to use our leverage—and to use it for a variety of purposes. I ticked off a series in my testimony, but I would identify what I consider to be the most important.

I think, A, we should be using it to ensure that the military really does go back to the barracks, to ensure that the interim government is empowered to make real decisions.

And along those lines, I think they should be working with the IMF, because the signal that sends, and finalize the standby agreement. I think there should be inclusiveness.

I think it should be a transparent political process. I think there should be international monitors who would be invited in to observe the elections, to demonstrate that these will be free and fair, even if it means that the timing should reflect the need for preparation for those elections.

I think, as well, there should be, the point you made about, I would say, pardoning the 43 NGOs who were arrested for violating Egyptian laws, I think that, in fact, they should be pardoned. I think one of the most important things we could do and the signal it would send about what Egypt's real posture is with regard to building a civil society, which is the key to having a level playing field and building the basis for free and fair elections, and creating the political space for political pluralism, we should use our leverage for those purposes and for allowing the Muslim Brotherhood to be included within elections as well. If they choose not to take part, let that be their decision.

The bottom line of what I am suggesting is, without having illusions about how much leverage we have, recognizing the limits of what they may be, we should not take ourselves out of the game right now. We should not be a bystander. We should not simply make a statement for the sake of making a statement. We should try to exercise the influence that we have, to shape the direction that Egypt takes.

We have a huge stake in how Egypt evolves. And I think, ultimately, we should exercise that leverage.

Understand the following, if, in fact, we find that we are not listened to, we can always cut off assistance later. I do not object to the use of assistance. I do not object to the idea that, in fact, we should be prepared to cut it off if we find that there is not responsiveness to the points and that principles that we are pushing. But if we were to do it at this point, I think that unfortunately we will no longer have an effect on what happens in Egypt.

And given our stakes, I do not think at this point we should cut ourselves off.

Thank you.

[The prepared statement of Ambassador Ross follows:]

PREPARED STATEMENT OF HON. DENNIS ROSS

Good morning Chairman Menendez, Ranking Member Corker, and distinguished committee members. I am pleased to appear before the committee again. The last time I appeared was to address Syria and the challenges of the civil war—challenges that affect our interests morally and strategically. Today, I am here to talk about the recent events in Egypt. While the nature of the challenge and our choices for responding are fundamentally different, there should be no mistaking that both our values and strategic interests are also very much at stake.

Egypt is the largest Arab country; historically, its influence has been felt politically and culturally throughout the region. It has often been the trendsetter or bellwether, and today its direction is sure to affect the shape of the Middle East.

The Arab Awakening may have begun in Tunisia, but it was Tahrir Square that captured the imagination of the region and much of the world. And it is again the events in Tahrir Square and elsewhere on Egyptian streets that a new, unsettling reality in Egypt is being created. A democratically elected leader was removed and is now under arrest. In Egypt itself, however, a majority seem to feel that this was the only possible option open to the Egyptian public. They saw a leader and his Muslim Brotherhood backers incapable of dealing with Egypt's problems and more focused on control than governance.

Though the claims may vary on how many people turned out on the streets of Cairo—with some estimates ranging as high as 13 to 14 million people—there is no disputing the fact that massive, unprecedented numbers of Egyptians demonstrated and called for the removal of a leadership that they saw leading their country to ruin. Many who had voted for President Morsi felt betrayed by his leadership that they saw as exclusionary, authoritarian, intolerant, and incompetent. The numbers that responded to the Tamarod (rebellion) petitions on recall, as well as to the call for demonstrations on June 30 to demand that Mohammad Morsi step down, are simply staggering. A critical mass of Egyptians signed the petitions and the opposition embodied all classes and walks of life. No doubt the economic breakdown, the rise in prices, electricity black and brown outs, the gas and breadlines, the absence of law and order—and the seeming indifference and inability of the Morsi-led government to address these daily problems of life—triggered much of the opposition.

It is not an exaggeration to describe what happened on June 30 as a popular uprising against the Morsi-led government—a popular revolt that the military used to remove the Egyptian President and crack down on the leadership of the Muslim Brotherhood. For many in the Middle East, this second Egyptian revolution constitutes an important course correction. Certainly, that explains why Saudi Arabia, the UAE, and Kuwait have pledged over $12 billion of assistance to Egypt, and they have already begun delivering on that assistance.

Others challenge this narrative of a popular uprising that triggered military intervention and the replacement of the Morsi-led, Muslim Brotherhood dominated government. They see not a course correction, but a democratically elected government removed by the Egyptian military. This is certainly the argument of the Muslim Brotherhood and their supporters in Egypt, and they hope to gain international support for their demand that Morsi be reinstated. They say they will not rest until he is reinstated and threaten to disrupt life in Egypt until this happens.

The United States is not the central player in the drama that is being played out in Egypt today. But we are also not a bystander. For understandable reasons, we must be deeply troubled when a democratically elected leader is removed not at the ballot box but by the military. In addition, it is hard to escape the reality that Egypt today is deeply polarized between those who support the removal of the Morsi-led government and those who oppose what they call a coup and the new interim civilian government that has now been appointed. The prospect of bridging this divide in the near term is very small. Though there are rumors of mediation efforts between the Brotherhood and the military or those in the new interim government, it is hard to see an agreement any time soon. The Brotherhood insists on Morsi's reinstatement and the military absolutely rejects such a possibility.

Some hold out hope that a compromise may yet be possible; one in which Morsi would be reinstated for a brief symbolic time, would then step down in favor of a technocratic interim government, and new elections would then take place for President. In an atmosphere in which there were both bridge builders and a readiness on the part of the main protagonists—the military and the Brotherhood—to reach a compromise, it might be possible. But such an environment does not exist today and is not going to exist any time soon.

Instead, the military and security forces have cracked down on the leaders of the Brotherhood, arrested hundreds of their followers, and closed down their media outlets—and they have done so with support and applause from much of the Egyptian public, including from many, but not all, liberal voices. In addition, a new civilian interim government has been named with no Islamists in it. Moreover, 11 of the 34 members of the new Cabinet served as ministers under Mubarak. The polarization is real. As much as we might inveigh against it, we should have no illusions that it is a temporary phenomenon.

The Muslim Brotherhood may speak of a coup and of democracy cheated. But in power, the Brotherhood did not act democratically. By appointing primarily members of the Brotherhood to key positions, issuing decrees to deny judicial oversight, pushing a law to remove 3,000 judges, drafting a constitution only with Islamists, rushing through a referendum on that constitution, using its thugs to brutalize protestors outside the Presidential Palace, prosecuting those who insulted the President, and failing to address a collapsing economy, the Brotherhood alienated a majority of the Egyptian public. This is not just the ''deep state'' reacting. This is not just a return of the ''feloul''—or Mubarak apparatchiks—resuming control.

The interim Cabinet led by Prime Minister Hazam El-Beblawi has a number of highly credible figures in it who don't represent the so-called deep state. Beblawi, himself, is a well-respected economist. Similarly, two of the Deputy Prime Ministers, Hossam Eissa and Ziad Bahaa El-Din, are genuine liberals, one a cofounder of the Constitution Party and the other a founding member of the Social Democratic Party. The Minister of Finance, Ahmed Galal, spent 18 years at the World Bank—and there are others whose background and experience qualify them as genuine technocrats. But, as noted above, there are also those who were part of the era of Mubarak governance. And General El-Sisi is not only the Defense Minister and Commander of the Military, he is also one of the Deputy Prime Ministers—something that adds to the suspicion that the military, for all its talk of not wanting to govern, is the force behind all decisionmaking.

At this point, there can be little doubt that the military is the key arbiter of events in Egypt. The question for us is what to do now. The last thing the United States wants to see is for Egypt to become a failed or failing state. Certainly, we would like to see Egypt proceed on a path that promotes a representative, inclusive, tolerant government that tackles its problems and respects minority and women's rights and fulfills its international obligations, including its peace treaty with Israel. The challenge for us is to adopt policies, recognizing the limits of our influence, that still offer more of a chance to see Egypt move in that direction.

Some argue that we should cut off assistance to Egypt. They say there was a coup; our law requires a cutoff; our principles demand it; and for the sake of consistency and credibility we should act accordingly. I respect this position but disagree with it. I don't do so easily. But I do so because I fear, at least at this juncture, that cutting off assistance would mean losing whatever leverage and influence we might be able to employ in Egypt today. Presently, the military is the most important actor in Egypt, and we must take into account that it has extensive public support.

The moment we cut off assistance, we not only will trigger a backlash from the military but also from a wide segment of the Egyptian public. We will be seen as trying to dictate to Egypt against the will of the people. Our claims of simply following our laws and our principles may ring true here but will not in Egypt. Nor will they have much resonance elsewhere in the region where the preoccupation remains largely centered on Syria and where the widely held perception is that America's principles don't seem to be guiding us there.

Furthermore, we should have no illusions: the Saudis and Emirates will be quick to fill in for lost American assistance at least in the near term. And while we may be focused on getting the Egyptian military and its new civilian government to exercise restraint and to be inclusive, the Saudis and Emirates will urge just the opposite. They see the Muslim Brotherhood and the rise of political Islam as a mortal threat and believe they must be suppressed—not included or treated as legitimate political participants.

In arguing against a cutoff of assistance, I am, at the same time, also arguing that we must use our leverage. Without exaggerating our leverage, it is fair to say we have some. The Egyptian military surely does not want us to cut our assistance in part because they have become dependent on U.S. weapons and a broad support structure—something that is in our mutual interests. But beyond wanting to avoid the practical consequences of seeing pipelines potentially cut and material supplies put on hold, the military also does not want us to lend credence to the Brotherhood's narrative of a coup. That would surely hurt Egypt's standing internationally—making meaningful assistance from others outside of the region far more difficult to obtain.

The real issue, therefore, is how to try to use our leverage and to what ends. Here I would focus on:

- Trying to get the military to truly go back to the barracks;
- Acting with restraint and minimizing their own use of violence;
- Ensuring that the interim government is empowered to make decisions and deal with real problems—and that means as an example not deferring discussions with the IMF but actually concluding them;
- Having the transition process be transparent;
- Emphasizing that only those who advocate violence would be excluded from the political process and elections;
- Committing to having international monitors come in to observe the elections, even if that requires less haste and more preparation for those elections;
- And, last, demonstrating a clear commitment to building civil society and its institutions.

This last point is critical. One of the clearest signs that the military and the interim government are serious about building a fair and open society and advancing the cause of representative government would be to pardon those representatives of those civil society groups who were found guilty of violating Egyptian laws. The military and interim government should act to revoke those laws and support the drafting of new ones that would permit NGOs to operate freely and effectively with financial support from inside and outside. If there are to be repeatable elections that are fairly contested and more likely to be respected—and a real space opened up for political pluralism—Egypt must build the institutions of civil society. We should use our leverage to press for this.

We should also press to permit the Muslim Brotherhood to participate in elections—assuming they are not encouraging their supporters to engage in violence. If they choose not to participate, let that be their decision.

None of this will happen easily, and there are no guarantees that even if we seek to use our leverage we will succeed. But cutting off the assistance now won't end up serving our interests or our values. Egypt's political future is bound to be messy and to move in fits and starts. We should try to use our leverage quietly for now, but there should be no doubt on the part of the military and the interim government that we will become more vocal and if there is no responsiveness, we will be prepared to cut off assistance.

I don't reject cutting off assistance or reshaping it in principle. I reject it now because I think it will backfire and not serve our hopes and aims for how Egypt should evolve. Our stakes in Egypt remain high. It makes sense for us to stay in the game and try to affect Egypt's course, and not make a statement that will render us largely irrelevant as Egyptians shape an uncertain future.

The CHAIRMAN. Thank you.

Dr. Dunne.

STATEMENT OF DR. MICHELE DUNNE, VICE PRESIDENT FOR THE ATLANTIC COUNCIL AND DIRECTOR OF THE RAFIK HARIRI CENTER FOR THE MIDDLE EAST, ATLANTIC COUNCIL, WASHINGTON, DC

Dr. DUNNE. Thank you, Chairman Menendez, Ranking Member Corker, and members of the committee. Thanks for the honor of testifying before this committee about the crisis in Egypt.

As we look at the political turmoil in Egypt and try to sort out United States policy options, I would like to raise for your consideration four points.

The first point is that the July 3 removal of Muslim Brotherhood President Mohamed Morsi by military coup, following enormous demonstrations, should not be understood primarily as a triumph of secularism over Islamism, because along with secularists and Islamists in Egypt, there is another major party, a third major player, which is the Egyptian State itself, which was left largely intact after the removal of former President Mubarak in February 2011.

So in the period after Mubarak ouster, the military, which is the most powerful player within the state, worked with Islamists and against the secularists. Now military, as well as other state institutions that have been on the defensive since the 2011 revolution, have aligned with the secular parties against the Brotherhood.

So we have to understand that the state is a major player here, and this new alignment may not be any more stable or lasting than the last one was.

It is also important to recognize that this current alliance between the military and other parts of the state with the secular opposition is anti-Brotherhood, but it is not anti-Islamist. The Salafi al-Nour Party supported the removal of Morsi and has already exerted its influence in the new transition by vetoing Cabinet choices and getting its preferred language on the Islamic sharia into the temporary constitution.

My second point is that we should really reserve judgment for now as to whether the removal of Morsi will put Egypt back on a path toward democracy or not. There are contradictory signs.

Now on the positive side of the ledger, the military is not exerting control directly, but has put civilians out front, unlike the first time they took control after Mubarak. And they put in place a Cabinet, as Ambassador Ross mentioned, of respected figures.

In addition to that, I would say another positive sign is that the new transition roadmap puts the rewriting of the constitution before the holding of new parliamentary and Presidential elections. And this does correct a flaw in the first transition, because the fact that they held elections before writing the new constitution the first time allowed the winners—that was the Brotherhood—to dominate the process and exclude others.

But on the negative side of the ledger, the way in which democratic process was cast aside on July 3 is troubling. Morsi was a failure as a President, and he behaved as though winning 52 percent of the vote gave him a mandate to rule as a pharaoh. And the broad public opposition to his leadership was real. But it would have been much more powerful and salutary for Egypt's young democracy if Morsi had been defeated in an early election or referendum.

There were some efforts made to persuade Morsi to accept this, but they were very, very brief, and then very quickly, the military moved to remove him in this way, in a way in which I think sets a dangerous precedent.

In addition to this, the new transition going on in Egypt is in danger of repeating the single most important mistake of the first transition, which was the failure to build a broad consensus and a tendency to exclude critical players. The secularists were excluded before. The Brotherhood is the being excluded now.

While Egyptian officials are speaking the language of inclusion, reconciliation, and dialogue, their actions are saying the opposite. As we know, President Morsi and a couple dozen other senior leaders of the Brotherhood are detained incommunicado without charge. There are rumors surfacing daily that they may be charged with some very serious offenses, such as treason or terrorism.

And there are lots of other signs, too, that the intention is to exclude the Brotherhood, perhaps outlaw it again, and so forth.

So there is a real contradiction here between the talk about inclusion and the actions that the government is taking.

My third point is, despite the military's argument that it took this action to remove Morsi in order to spare the country a civil war, Egypt, in fact, seems to be headed into a period of greater instability and that perhaps a cycle of instability.

There has already been a troubling spike in violence, more than 160 people killed and 1,400 injured in just the first couple of weeks; daily clashes between pro- and anti-Morsi groups throughout the country, and of course Egypt is a much more heavily armed country than it was a couple years ago; and a spike in jihad attacks against the military and police officers in the Sinai and also now in other parts of Egypt.

Egypt could easily, in this situation, see a return to the type of insurgency and domestic terrorism it experienced in the 1990s when jihadis targeted government officials, Christians, tourists, and liberals.

If there is this kind of ongoing violence, it will not be possible to attract tourists and investment back to Egypt, and all the good intentions to now rebuild the economy, and all the money, even, coming into the central bank from gulf donors and so forth, will not work to revitalize the economy, if the security situation continues to deteriorate.

And the call yesterday by Deputy Prime Minister El-Sisi, the Defense Minister, for massive demonstrations tomorrow in order to provide him, he said, a mandate to crack down on terrorism I think risks escalating the situation and the violence further.

My fourth point is this, in light of all these many dangers, the United States should proceed with caution and be guided by some basic principles.

Egypt can only be a reliable security partner for the United States and a reliable peace partner for Israel if it is reasonably stable. And it will only become stable once it develops a governing system that answers strong and persistent popular demands for responsiveness, accountability, fairness, and respect for citizens' right.

So we are going to have to look at the signs in the coming weeks about whether there really will be inclusiveness or whether this campaign of excluding the Brotherhood will escalate. Will there be things like media freedom, civil society, freedom? Ambassador Ross mentioned this very important case against 43 NGO workers, including 16 Americans who have been convicted and sentenced to prison for NGO work in Egypt. So we are going to have to look at these signs.

During this time, the United States should take this time to pause, suspend military deliveries and assistance in accordance with our law, and review our policy toward Egypt and our assistance to Egypt, including special privileges that Egypt receives, such as cash flow financing for foreign military financing.

The United States should carry out its own internal review as well as a dialogue with Egyptians inside and outside the Egyptian Government with the stated intention of resuming assistance as soon as the country is clearly back on a democratic path.

In the meantime, we really should do a review of the kind of military and economic assistance we offer Egypt, which should not be kept on autopilot, but rather updated in order to provide the kind of assistance, when it is resumed, that is truly suitable to promoting a stable, prosperous, democratic Egypt that plays a vital and responsible role in the Middle East.

The United States is understandably wary of damaging its long-standing relationship with the Egyptian Government. But it should also avoid pursuing a policy that appears to be cynical and unprincipled.

We should not make the mistake of concluding that the United States no longer has any influence in Egypt. In fact, the fact that Egyptians pay such close attention to what our officials say, and have been very critical of our policy, means, actually, that we still have quite a lot of influence to exert.

Thank you.

[The prepared statement of Dr. Dunne follows:]

PREPARED STATEMENT OF DR. MICHELE DUNNE

Chairman Menendez, Ranking Member Corker, members of the committee, thank you for the honor of testifying before this committee about the crisis in Egypt. As we analyze the political turmoil in Egypt and try to sort out U.S. policy options, I would like to raise four points for your consideration.

First, the July 3 removal of Muslim Brotherhood President Mohammed Morsi by military coup following enormous demonstrations should not be understood primarily as a triumph of secularism over Islamism. Along with secularists and Islamists, there is a third major player in Egyptian politics: the state itself, which was left largely intact after the removal of former President Hosni Mubarak in February 2011. In the period after Mubarak's ouster, the military (the most powerful player within the state) worked with the Islamists and against the secular opposition. Now the military, as well as other state institutions that were on the defense after the 2011 revolution, have allied with the secular parties against the Brotherhood. So what has happened is in part a reassertion of the Mubarak era state, a sort of counterrevolution.

In addition, it is important to recognize that the current state-secularist alliance is anti-Brotherhood but not necessarily anti-Islamist. The Salafi Nour Party supported the removal of Morsi and has already exerted its influence by vetoing cabinet choices and getting its preferred wording on the status of Islamic sharia into the temporary constitution.

Second, the United States should reserve judgment for now as to whether the removal of Morsi will put Egypt back on a path toward democracy or not. It is too soon to tell and the signs are contradictory. On the positive side of the ledger, the military is not exerting control directly but rather has put civilians out front, including a President from the judiciary and a Cabinet including respected technocrats and well known secular political figures. The Cabinet is particularly well placed to address the economy, which is in dire straits. And the new transition roadmap puts the rewriting of the constitution before the holding of new parliamentary and Presidential elections. This corrects a major flaw of the first transition in which constitution-writing followed elections, allowing the winners to dominate the process and exclude the losers.

On the negative side of the ledger, the way in which the democratic process was cast aside on July 3 is troubling. Morsi was a failure as a President, who behaved as though winning 52 percent of the vote gave him a mandate to rule as a pharaoh. The broad public opposition to his leadership was real, seen in the millions who signed a petition for early elections and poured into the streets on June 30. But it would have been much more powerful and salutary for Egypt's young democracy if Morsi had been defeated in an early election or referendum; instead, his removal from office by the military shortly after protests began sets a dangerous precedent. Instead of learning the lesson that ineffective and undemocratic governance brings a comeuppance at the ballot box, the Brotherhood and others Islamists have learned that playing the democratic game by the rules does not pay off.

In addition, the new transition is in danger of repeating the most important mistake of the earlier post-Mubarak stage, which was a failure to build a broad consensus because critical players were excluded from important decisions. Before the July 3 removal of Morsi it was the secular liberals and leftists who were excluded; now it is the Muslim Brotherhood. Egypt is moving into a period in which one of the most deeply rooted movements in the country's political life might be excluded, perhaps severely repressed or at a minimum strongly disadvantaged, just as the secularists were until recently.

While Egyptian officials are speaking the language of inclusion and reconciliation, their actions toward the Muslim Brotherhood are saying the opposite. In addition to Mohammed Morsi, an undisclosed number—perhaps two dozen—of senior leaders of the Brotherhood and its Freedom and Justice Party are detained incommunicado without charge, with new rumors surfacing daily about serious crimes with which they might be charged, including treason. They have been banned from travel and their assets seized. The Brotherhood-dominated upper House of Parliament has been dissolved, and the new transition government is busy expunging Brotherhood appointees from bodies such as the Supreme Press Council and National Council for Human Rights. And there is talk of outlawing the Brotherhood itself, which only recently gained license as a nongovernmental organization.

Third, despite the military's argument that it spared the country a civil war, Egypt might well be headed into greater instability. The new transition might once again produce a constitution and elected bodies that a significant part of the population considers illegitimate, leading to repeated political breakdowns, resets, and military intervention in politics—a cycle of instability. Already there has been a troubling spike in violence, with more than 160 killed and 1,400 injured in demonstrations, daily clashes between pro- and anti-Morsi groups throughout the country, and hundreds arrested. Jihadi attacks against military and police officers in the Sinai have increased sharply, with more than 20 officers killed in the past 2 weeks. With Islamists rethinking the value of peaceful political participation, Egypt could easily see a return to the type of insurgency and domestic terrorism it experienced in the 1990s, when jihadis targeted government officials, Christians, and tourists. Under those circumstances, it will not be possible to attract tourists and investment back to Egypt in the numbers needed to revitalize the economy.

Fourth, in light of these many dangers, the United States should proceed with caution and be guided by basic principles. Egypt can only be a reliable security partner for the United States and peace partner for Israel if it is reasonably stable, and it will only become stable once it develops a governing system that answers strong popular demands for responsiveness, accountability, fairness, and respect for citizens' rights.

There will be signs in the coming weeks showing in which direction Egypt is moving after this cataclysmic change. Will Morsi and other Brotherhood leaders be released and encouraged to participate in peaceful politics, or will they be imprisoned on trumped-up charges? Will there be freedom for the media, including those affiliated with the Brotherhood? Will the process to amend the constitution be broadly inclusive, or will it be rushed, nontransparent, and designed to meet the demands of a chosen few, such as the military and the Salafis? Will Egyptian and foreign nongovernmental organizations be given freedom to operate and serve as watchdogs of the transition, and will the recent convictions of 43 NGO workers (including 16 Americans) be reversed?

The United States should take this time to pause, suspend military deliveries and assistance in accordance with our law, and review policy toward and assistance to Egypt, including special privileges such as cash flow financing for Foreign Military Financing. The U.S. administration should carry out its own internal review as well as a broad dialogue with Egyptians inside and outside the government, with the stated intention of resuming assistance as soon as the country is clearly back on a democratic path. Military and economic assistance should not be kept on autopilot as they were during the Mubarak years, but updated in order to support a stable, prosperous, democratic Egypt that plays a vital and responsible role in the Middle East region.

The United States is understandably wary of damaging its longstanding relationship with the Egyptian Government and military, but it should also avoid pursuing a policy that appears cynical and unprincipled. Hewing too closely to the party currently in power, treating opposition groups and civil society as irrelevant, and ignoring democratic principles have earned the United States sharp criticism from all sides in Egypt. But we should not make the mistake of concluding that the United States no longer has any influence there; the fact that Egyptians still pay such close attention to what our officials and diplomats do and say suggests quite the opposite.

The CHAIRMAN. Thank you.
Ambassador Kurtzer.

STATEMENT OF HON. DANIEL C. KURTZER, S. DANIEL ABRA-IIAM PROFESSOR IN MIDDLE EASTERN POLICY STUDIES, WOODROW WILSON SCHOOL OF PUBLIC AND INTERNA-TIONAL AFFAIRS, PRINCETON UNIVERSITY, PRINCETON, NJ

Ambassador KURTZER. Mr. Chairman, Ranking Member Senator Corker, distinguished members of the committee, thank you very much for the invitation to be here today.

And to you, Senator Menendez, as a citizen of New Jersey, thank you for your service on behalf of all of us and for our Nation.

Having spent 7 years living in Egypt while serving our country in our Foreign Service, I cannot tell you how excited I have been over these past 2 years to see a people long under the yoke of authoritarianism and dictatorship striving to define who it is they are and what it is they want to be, how they want to shape their society.

In fact, this has been largely a revolution to define Egypt's identity and to establish a constitutional basis, a legal basis, for Egypt to pursue its own form of democracy.

In some respects, then, what we are experiencing today is the second chance for this revolution, a revolution that has gone through a number of phases and is likely to continue to go through phases, as the Egyptians wrestle with these pressing large issues on their agenda.

I would offer, then, three comments in addition to the written testimony that I submitted for the record.

First, we need to understand that this is an ongoing, dynamic process. We are in round three or four of what might be termed a heavyweight bout. There are forces in Egypt that are going to continue to contest for political power. And the Egyptian public is, as we know, badly divided, almost evenly divided, among these various forces, including those who look to the military and security services for stability and law and order, including those who would like to see Egypt defined by an Islamist agenda, and including those who were not that unhappy with the previous regime and simply want to return to some form of stability while enjoying some more liberty and freedom.

So we need to be patient as a revolution that is only in its 3rd year continues. And as revolutions go, they normally take a long time to unfold.

I think, second, as we look at the events, particularly over the last few weeks in Egypt, we should be struck by the degree to which a form of popular will was expressed, both in the petition that gathered many millions of signatures, as well as the demonstrations on June 30 and afterward that persuaded the military to oust former President Mohammad Morsi.

I know we are debating the question of whether this fits the definition of a coup, according to our law, and we should be debating that question, as the lawyers look at legal issues. But we also need to be mindful that millions of Egyptians took to the street from all classes, all sectors of society, not just Cairo, but upper Egypt as well, Alexandria and the delta, to say that they did not like what President Mohammad Morsi was doing to the country, having ignored the advice of experts on the economy, having fired judges and basically asserted powers and accrued powers only to himself, having turned a blind eye when it came to massacres of Coptic Christians and others.

In other words, the Egyptian people basically said we were ready to go to the streets to push Hosni Mubarak out of office, and we were ready to go the streets to push Mohammad Morsi out of office. And so that popular will also needs to be factored into our thinking.

And the third point I would note, in line with previous testimony of my colleagues, is the question of U.S. leverage. I think we need to understand that the Egypt-United States relationship that we have enjoyed now for more than three decades is changing, and it is changing rather rapidly. The degree to which our assistance in the late 1970s and 1980s and 1990s contributed to major changes in Egypt: we helped transform the Egyptian military from a military reliant upon Soviet doctrine, training, and weapons, to a military that is basically interoperable with ours.

That military provides significant strategic assistance to whatever we do in the Middle East and beyond the Middle East, as we know.

We have created a partnership with Egyptian intelligence and counterterrorism agencies that has been of direct benefit to the

United States in our own effort to counter terrorism against us and against our interests.

We helped changed the Egyptian economy from the statist economy that Hosni Mubarak inherited in 1981 to an economy which is largely dominated by the private sector, although there are still changes that need to be effected to make this an economy that provides its benefits fairly to all the Egyptian people.

In other words, the investment that we made in Egypt over the past decades has paid off. And it is an investment that we need to consider as we think about what we want to do in the future.

Our leverage with respect to Egypt today is reduced, and we need to understand that. And the degree to which we do can help us see Egypt through what some are calling a second chance in its own revolution, but a second chance also for us to redefine this important strategic relationship.

In that respect, I think it would be shortsighted to cut aid to the Egyptian military at this time. In fact, as I say in my written testimony, we should have considered doing this years ago, because Egypt's needs have largely been economic, our having helped transform their military to a military that is interoperable with ours.

But to cut that aid off now would lose us the one partner that has proven to be stable and reliable in pursuit of our own strategic objectives.

So right now, our objective should be to see Egypt through this crisis, to help it by providing advice quietly. We tend to say too much publicly in this country. We tend to react too much to daily events. We tend not to sit back and see how trends are going. And so quiet advice may be the order of the day.

And secondly, I think our own actions in this respect need to be tempered as well, understanding that the Egyptian people, a proud people, are going to define their own future. We can help them do it, but we cannot make demands of them and expect them to follow our demands simply because we are providing assistance.

Thank you, Mr. Chairman.

[The prepared statement of Ambassador Kurtzer follows:]

PREPARED STATEMENT OF HON. DANIEL C. KURTZER

Current situation in Egypt

Egypt remains in a state of revolutionary upheaval, marked by political, economic, and social instability. Since the ouster of former President Hosni Mubarak in February 2011, Egypt's political parties and groupings have been beset by severe internal wrangling, and they remain badly fractured. Successive administrations have failed to establish security and basic law and order, and have also failed to secure enough political consensus from opposing political forces so as to be able to govern effectively.

Ousted President Mohamed Morsi faced, and could not resolve, pressing problems: A breakdown in law and order, especially acute in the Sinai Peninsula; depleted foreign exchange holdings, exacerbated by slowdowns in key economic sectors; and food and energy shortages. Morsi's own actions contributed to significant doubts about his and the Muslim Brotherhood's agenda, sparking fear of a rapid Islamicization of Egypt. He fired judges, paid little heed to violence against Coptic Christians, rammed through a new constitution, failed to take any steps to remedy the economic crisis, and seized nearly all powers in his own hands. Because the election to the People's Assembly (Parliament) had been nullified by the courts, no mechanism existed constitutionally to challenge Morsi's rule. In place of an unavailable impeachment process, a civil society organization, Tamarod, organized an unprecedented mass petition and mass rallies involving an estimated 20 million Egyptians throughout the country, representing all classes and social strata. This led the military to oust Morsi in early July and install an interim civilian-led administration.

The interim government is now in place, and it is the strongest and most reputable since 2011. The government is reaching out to the Muslim Brotherhood to try to launch a national reconciliation process, but the Brotherhood thus far is demanding conditions—such as the restoration to office of Morsi—that are unacceptable to both the government and the military. The government has also promised a rapid return to constitutional rule, including a process for amending and approving a revised constitutions and new elections for President and the Parliament.

Viability of the interim government's roadmap to restore democratic government

The new Cabinet faces at least four daunting challenges: To stabilize the internal situation and restore law and order, thus providing a much-needed sense of security for Egyptians to return to normal life; to find a pathway to political reconciliation with the Muslim Brotherhood, thus preventing a possible spiral of violence between supporters of the government and army and supporters of the Brotherhood; to kick-start the economy which has been stalled since the 2011 revolution, a task made easier by an injection of substantial Arab aid and loans; and to organize a fair, transparent process of amending the constitution and conducting new elections for President and Parliament.

Of these urgent requirements, the most challenging will be the reintegration of the Muslim Brotherhood into the political process. Mutual distrust, the desire for settling scores, and long-term antipathy between the Brotherhood and the military complicate this process. The interim government reportedly has reached out to the Brotherhood, but the Brotherhood's preconditions—to restore Morsi to the Presidency, reaffirm the constitution, and reinstate the Shura Council—have been a stumbling block, perhaps insurmountable. In the meantime, the Brotherhood continues to mobilize demonstrations of its own, and it is surely capable to doing violent things.

In this standoff between the Brotherhood and the military, each counts on a strong base of support. The Brotherhood has long experience in maintaining its internal base, having spent much of its 85 years underground. But the Brotherhood has lost ground in the past year, and is now more hard-pressed to demonstrate the political clout that brought its leadership to power during the past 2 years.

On the other hand, it is widely accepted in Egypt since the 1952 revolution that the military is the most important symbol and embodiment of modern Egyptian nationalism. The liberal parties that flourished in Egypt before the 1952 revolution proved unable to govern, stand up to British domination, or deal with the corruption of the monarchy. For the past decades, the military has been content, in the words of Dr. Steven Cook, to "rule" but not "govern," that is, it sees itself as the ultimate arbiter of power in the country but does not want to govern day to day. Indeed, the military's poor governing performance after the 2011 revolution reinforced the preference to sit behind, rather than on, the seat of power.

It is possible, surely desirable, that this state of affairs change over time, as Egypt's very nascent democracy matures. For this change to happen, Egypt needs to develop more mature democratic institutions and a more tolerant democratic political culture and atmosphere. This is simply not the situation today.

Prospects for further political and civil unrest

Increasingly violent confrontations between the Muslim Brotherhood and the security forces, as well as the serious breakdown of law and order in the Sinai Peninsula, almost guarantee that things will remain unstable in Egypt for some time. Even if the interim government can induce the Brotherhood to enter reconciliation talks, the government will require a strong, coercive capacity to ensure domestic calm. Absent this, the violence could easily deteriorate over time into civil war.

In this respect, it would make no sense for the United States to cut off aid to the Egyptian military, the one group in Egypt that continues to share our interests and the only group ultimately capable of assuring domestic stability. The standing of the United States in Egypt today is as low as it has been at any time since the days of Gamal Abdel Nasser. A cutoff of assistance now would gain nothing for the United States, but would surely alienate us from the military.

American national security interests in Egypt

The United States has important national security interests in Egypt:

• Military cooperation and coordination: Virtually everyone and everything the U.S. military sends to Afghanistan and the gulf passes through or over Egypt, and Egyptian military coordination/cooperation is vital to the execution of our

military's missions. The Egyptians provide vital, expedited Suez Canal clearances, and facilities for the repair and refueling of our planes and equipment.
- Intelligence cooperation: Egypt and the United States maintain a robust and mutually beneficial intelligence relationship.
- Antiterrorism cooperation: Egypt has been a significant partner in the United States effort to push back against global terrorism.
- Peace process: The Egyptian-Israeli peace treaty remains the cornerstone of efforts to achieve a comprehensive peace, and Egypt's support for Palestinian peacemaking efforts remains vital.
- Regional politics: While Egypt's leadership role in Arab and Muslim politics has softened in recent years, its influence remains in moderate politics in   the region.
- Democratic change: Notwithstanding all the challenges noted above, Egypt's slow and unsteady march toward democracy continues to represent a very important model for the rest of the region, in either its possible success or failure.

Options for U.S. foreign policy to support the restoration of democracy, including the appropriate role of U.S. foreign assistance

There is a story, possibly apocryphal, of a Soviet general who was asked in 1972 whether the Soviets were upset about Sadat's decision to expel Soviet military advisers from Egypt. "Certainly," the general replied, "we are upset about losing our foothold in Egypt. But remember, we enjoyed 17 years of strategic friendship . . . not bad."

It is extremely hard for global actors to maintain a strategic relationship with regional states over a long period of time. Not only do their interests fail to align properly, but there are great incentives for both to play off the other in a constantly shifting environment of regional and global politics. The U.S.-Egyptian relationship is entering its 45th year—a remarkable achievement in and of itself.

That said, no relationship can remain static in the face of changes in the environment. Although Egypt continues to face security challenges—Sinai, Ethiopia water, regional conflict spillover—a reasonable (nonprofessional) assessment is that Egypt could sustain a gradual, steady diminution in U.S. military assistance. Indeed, it would have made sense years ago to shift U.S. aid gradually from military to economic assistance; and it will make sense to do so in the future, after the domestic political and economic situation stabilizes. Today, however, Egypt's emergency economic and financial needs are acute. The successful conclusion of an IMF agreement should stimulate substantial external assistance, including from the United States; and, as noted above, it is vital to maintain our relationship with the military.

Morsi's ouster was not a preference of American policy, just as Morsi's actions while in office were not consistent with American interests. The reality is our bilateral relationship has changed, and the leverage and the influence the United States used to exercise in Egypt no longer are as potent. But in the same way that current events represent a second chance for the Egyptian revolution to succeed, they also represent a strategic opportunity for the United States to stabilize and strengthen our relationship with Egypt, and to preserve important American interests.

The CHAIRMAN. Well, thank you all for your testimony. It is very insightful.

And as both diplomats and academics, you need more than 5 minutes to do it, but it was all very worthwhile.

Let me start off. I am concerned, and I would like to hear your views, I think Egyptian society believes that the United States somehow sided with the Brotherhood in a way that was against their will. And I sense that from conversations, from civil society, from reading.

And if we were to cut off the aid now, would that not, in that civil society, reinforce the view that that is, in fact, the position of the United States? What would you say to that?

Ambassador ROSS. Yes, I do think that would be the effect. Whether the perception was correct or not is immaterial. It existed.

And if now we were seen as cutting off aid, it would be seen as being a statement that we were siding with the Brotherhood against, as I said, what I think is a majority of the public. I am not saying it is a wide majority, but I think it is a majority of the public, and we would be seen as trying to dictate against the popular will.

So I think it would produce a backlash. It would not yield us any benefit. And that is one of the reasons I do not favor it.

The CHAIRMAN. Anyone else want to venture a comment?

Dr. DUNNE. Senator Menendez, you are quite correct that a lot of Egyptians think the United States sided with the Brotherhood. And before that, they thought we sided with the Supreme Council of the Armed Forces. So we have had a situation where Egyptians of all kinds, whether they are secular or Islamists, take a dim view of U.S. policy because they view it as having been without principle and narrowly self-serving, that we stuck close to Mubarak when he was in power, then the SCAF when they were in power, then Morsi when he was in power, and there have not been any principles motivating our policies. So that is one issue.

The other issue is how would Egyptians react to a suspension of our aid. I agree that what Ambassador Ross says is a danger, but it will depend largely on how the Egyptian military would decide to play this. They can drum up anti-U.S. sentiment, if they would like to.

Or they could choose to say, look, the United States is suspending this assistance temporarily. That is their law. But we are going to see through a democratic transition. And so it is not a problem. The assistance undoubtedly will be resumed, because we fully intend to come through on the transition to democracy.

Ambassador KURTZER. I would add one thing. First of all, to underscore what Dr. Dunne said, the fact is that the Egyptian public is perceiving American policy only in line with its own views. So when the SCAF, the Supreme Council of the Armed Forces, was in power, we were seen as holding them together. When the Muslim Brotherhood came to power, we were seen as supporting them. And we are now seen as supporting this interim government.

So trying to play to the sentiments of a public that is trying to sort out its own political views is going to be quite difficult.

Among the problems, though, in terms of this aid cutoff question, as you suggested, Senator, are the implications. And it is not just an implication defined by how the public would absorb this, or even, as Dr. Dunne suggested, how the military might react to it, but whether or not it serves our interests.

What is the military doing today that does serve our interests? They are trying to calm the situation in the Sinai Peninsula, which is extraordinarily dangerous, in which jihadists not only from Gaza, but from elsewhere, have fought to use that peninsula as a launching pad for attacks against Egyptians and against Israel.

They are also closing tunnels, tunnels that are used for smuggling between Sinai and Gaza. For the first time in decades, those tunnels are now in jeopardy.

And the military, as it is doing that, continues to provide the support that we have needed to move our personnel and our equipment where they have to go. And as long as we have deployments east of Egypt, we are going to require support and assistance from the Egyptian military to do so.

So in the short term, it may be that the military could live with a temporary cutoff. But we would be cutting off our own nose to spite our face, in this case. And I think it would not serve American interests to do that.

The CHAIRMAN. It seems to me that the question is some leverage versus no leverage, at the end of the day. And personally, I believe using the leverage is an appropriate use of American resources in pursuing the national interests of security of the United States.

I also think about cutting off aid totally at this time, as some have suggested, I know some of our colleagues, including some members of this committee, at a time in which Egypt's economy is in a downward spiral, and the potential effect of that. There may be others in the gulf who will try to replace us, which of course would mean we would have no influence. They would replace to some degree the assistance.

But it still would be, I think, a very significant blow to the economy. Is that an additional concern?

And secondly, some of the language in the appropriation bills that are beginning to move are citing three conditions for the disbursement of United States military assistance to Egypt. One is an inclusive political process; two is credible democratic elections; and three is democratic governance that protects the rights of religious minorities and women.

Do you think that those are the appropriate conditions? And precisely what steps should the military and the interim government take to satisfactorily check those three boxes?

Ambassador ROSS. Let me say a couple things.

First, I do think it has a potential on the economy, not just in terms of the objective reality, but what I would call psychologically, it has some potential impact. But I would worry, in a larger sense, less about the economy and more about our ability to affect the Egyptian military to exercise restraint.

I am worried, based again on what General El-Sisi said yesterday, that if we have little influence on the situation and they turn more to the gulf, understand one thing, the Saudis and Emirates, for their own reasons, want a very tough suppression of the Muslim Brotherhood because they see the Muslim Brotherhood and political Islam as a mortal threat to them.

So if we are, in effect, going to push the Egyptian military closer to the arms of the Gulf States, then I think any prospect of restraint goes out the window. And if part of our aim is to try to enhance the prospect of Egypt evolving over time in much more favorable direction, I think if we take ourselves out of this equation right now, the prospect of restraint disappears.

I would also say one other thing. I agree with something Dan said earlier. We are more likely to have an effect if we try to do it quietly. The more it appears, in the eyes of Egyptians, we are seen as telling them what to do, the more we may trigger a nationalist backlash.

Now, that does not mean we take away the potential to say things quietly, or it does not mean we take away the potential to say things publicly. They should understand what we say in private is not going to remain in private if there is no responsiveness. And they should understand they do lose a connection to us. And they want that connection to us.

But I am afraid if we do it in a way that they see as too heavy-handed, it will be used against us. And there is a long history here of the United States saying certain things in public that trigger a nationalist impulse.

I go back to the mid-1960s, when Nasser reacted to something President Johnson said, and said we could go drink all the water of the Mediterranean and the Red Sea.

The CHAIRMAN. Do either one of you want to——

Ambassador KURTZER. Yes, if I could comment on the economic crisis that Egypt is facing as part of your question, Senator.

I think you are exactly right that our focus on military assistance has to do with the legislation and the definition of what happened. But Egypt has been in economic crisis for the 2 years since the revolution began, which is quite ironic because if you look at the numbers just before the revolution, Egypt was on a very significant upward turn, with respect to its manufacturing sector and its tourism sector and its foreign exchange earnings.

They are now at a point where the gap in financing is approaching $3 billion a month. And in a situation where their foreign exchange has been depleted, and is declining rapidly, this represents a very significant crisis.

So as I suggested in my written testimony, there may be a need, in fact, if Egypt can reach agreement with the International Monetary Fund, to think about emergency assistance for Egypt to complement what the Arab States are doing in order to get Egypt over the economic hump.

On the second issue you raised, Senator, of the potential conditionality that is being written into legislation, as one who lived in Egypt for 7 years and worked with Egyptians for a very long time, when they hear about conditionality, even if the conditions support and complement what they want to do, their backs get up, and they become very challenged by it.

I hope we can talk about these as goals that we and the Egyptians share, the goals for an inclusive political process, a process in which the rights of women and minorities are protected.

To the extent, however, that these become the equivalent of dictates from the United States, I think we are going to see pushback from the Egyptians. And that will present its own kind of problem for us.

The CHAIRMAN. Thank you very much.

Let me——

Dr. DUNNE. Senator, may I comment on this question as well?

The CHAIRMAN. You know, I would like to move to other members. But I appreciate maybe at the end, when other members have had their opportunity.

Let me, before I turn to Senator Corker, recognize and welcome to the committee in his first hearing, Senator Markey of Massachusetts.

Senator Markey has a long history in the House of Representatives, where I had the privilege of serving with him. He has cared about international issues for some time and has been a leader in climate change and nuclear issues. And we welcome him to the committee and look forward to his service with us.

Senator Corker.

Senator CORKER. Thank you, Mr. Chairman.

And welcome, Senator.

And, Dr. Dunne, since we have such new spirit in the air here, if you want to take 30 seconds of my time to answer, go ahead.

Dr. DUNNE. Thank you, Senator.

Senator Menendez said it is a question of some leverage versus no leverage. The United States has kept the military assistance going and has never used it as leverage. So I think we are reaching a point where, really, there is not much credibility here of having any leverage with that assistance.

Ambassador Ross said he would be in favor of using it at some future point, if there was no responsiveness. My understanding is that the administration reached out rather assertively to General El-Sisi to argue against a military coup, and there was no responsiveness, so we are already at that point.

Senator CORKER. Thank you.

And, Mr. Chairman, again, thanks for having this hearing.

For what it is worth, I appreciate the testimony greatly. I do think that our Nation's role in Egypt right now should be an instrument of calmness. And I think all too often, we make these issues about us and what we are going to do—I mean, unfortunately, that is one of the great diseases we have here in Washington—when really this is about them, and it is about an orderly transition, and hopefully moving through a democratic process.

So I appreciate the comments relative to that, and think that that should be our role as we move forward.

And I agree that much of our advice should be happening privately and not so much divisiveness occurring here. So I very much appreciate the comments regarding that.

Let me ask you this question, the transition plan that has been put in place by the military, do we view that timeframe as something that is realistic?

Ambassador ROSS. I made a reference in my testimony to international observers, monitors coming in, and that if the international community, in terms of observing elections, were to say more time is necessary to prepare, I would actually favor that as it relates to the elections.

I do agree with what Michele said. Preparing the constitution in advance of elections is the right thing. It was important, I think, to put out a date for elections, but, again, I would like it to be guided more by the right kind of preparation above anything else.

Senator CORKER. Do you think it is somewhat unrealistic?

Ambassador ROSS. I am a little worried, just as I thought the way the SCAF approached things, it was not necessarily realistic. I think the sequence is more appropriate this time than it was last time.

But I still would like the ground to be prepared, and I would like to create more of a basis, potentially, for inclusion, which I think at this point is going to be very difficult to produce.

Senator CORKER. Dr. Dunne.

Dr. DUNNE. I agree with Ambassador Ross. I think the sequencing is good, but we also have a situation in which the constitution is to be rewritten by a small, closed committee and then looked at by 50 people appointed by the President. And it is also supposed to happen in just a couple months. I think it is probably unrealistic.

And if Egypt wants to have a constitution, which this time around you have much broader buy-in than last time, it is probably going to take longer and need to involve a lot more people.

Senator CORKER. Before moving to Mr. Kurtzer, you made the comment, I think, that the Muslim Brotherhood was not included. We have talked with many people in Egypt who say they have tried to include them in this process and have been spurned. So which is it?

Dr. DUNNE. Well, as I said, Senator, I think there are conflicting signals. I mean, people are saying the Muslim Brotherhood is included, is invited to dialogue. But then they have their entire leadership in prison, and so forth.

You know, Morsi also kept inviting the opposition to dialogue during his Presidency, but they knew that it was not a real and sincere offer and that he had no intention of really acting on that.

So unfortunately, this is something that is happening again and again in Egypt.

Senator CORKER. Well, Mr. Kurtzer, are they included or are they not? And what about the transition time?

Ambassador KURTZER. Well, on the transition time, Senator, we cannot have it both ways. On the one hand, we are pushing very hard for the military to truly go back to the barracks, which we all favor. And I think the military would prefer to do that as well. And on the other hand, we cannot complain about a short transition period. I think we are going to have to abide by Egyptian will in this case.

Now, it is a very fast, perhaps too fast, process that they are expecting. The whole thing is supposed to happen in 4 or 5 months, as these committees go through their work.

But if we want the military truly to go back to the barracks, then we may just have to buy into a process which is moving a little bit faster than we would advise.

With respect to the Muslim Brotherhood, the system is not going to stabilize unless some kind of a dialogue is undertaken successfully.

Senator CORKER. Do you think there has been the appropriate reach-out to try to include them in what is happening in this transition and they have spurned it, or not?

Ambassador KURTZER. Well, there have been efforts so far to reach out. So far, the pushback has been there as well.

One of the preconditions on the Muslim Brotherhood side is the release of former President Morsi. That may not happen soon.

But I would not doubt that there is dialogue underway every day behind the scenes, even as they are confronting each other in the street. The question is whether or not they are going to find a formula that will allow the Muslim Brotherhood to climb down from the tree, and also allow the military to climb down.

In this respect, we saw before the ouster of Morsi that the European Union, with its diplomats, had actually come quite close to persuading the Morsi government to undertake some reforms. It may be that there are also diplomatic activities going on behind the scenes in this direction.

Senator CORKER. Before stepping back to the bigger picture, if I have time, we read this morning about what is happening at the border crossing. I was in Rafah in Gaza not long ago, and to act as if there is actually border control was a joke. I mean, anything you wanted was coming through the tunnels. It was very sophisticated.

All of a sudden, the military has moved to close that off, which is a huge change in activity there.

Do we have any idea what is driving that abrupt, I would say, good change? But what is driving that?

Ambassador Ross. I think it is being driven by a couple of factors, but it all revolves around the perception of the military of Hamas and what Hamas has been doing.

There is a narrative that has built up in Egypt that Hamas has been very active within Egypt itself. And I think there is also perception that this movement through the tunnels was a two-way movement, and, therefore, it threatened Egypt. And you have jihadis now in the Sinai, and I think part of the closing of the tunnels is trying to affect that two-way traffic.

Ambassador KURTZER. There is also, Senator, a backstory that is emerging. There is a Reuters piece that I saw this morning that suggests that the military some months ago asked Morsi for approval to undertake a major security operation in Sinai. And Morsi's response, according to this article, was that he would not authorize actions by Muslims against Muslims.

So the military has been stymied in its effort to try to restore security in Sinai, and I think we are now seeing the first effort by the military to do what it wanted to do over the past year.

Senator CORKER. Thank you for your testimony and for being here.

Mr. Chairman, I will wait until the next round.

The CHAIRMAN. Thank you.

Senator Boxer.

Senator BOXER. Thank you so much, Senator Menendez, Senator Corker, for this opportunity to listen to people who are experts on this.

And I will tell you, we need to hear you, because so much of the situation is nuanced. And so cutting through that nuance is sometimes difficult, if you are not very familiar with it.

I just would like to say, to Dr. Dunne, on the issue of whether aid to Egypt gives us leverage, I am not asking a question, I am giving an opinion, which you do not have to share. But I think all of our foreign aid, being done for all the right reasons, humanitarian, and so on, it is still leverage.

I mean, we would hope that people would appreciate the fact that we care enough about them, and might, in fact, listen to us from our standpoint as to the best way to develop and the best way to reach for democracy.

So I would say I disagree with you. I think all of our foreign aid should give us leverage in the best of ways.

I wonder whether any of you would disagree with this, that Mubarak was a military dictator. Does anyone disagree with that on the panel?

So you all agree. He was a dictator, a military dictator. And he was in power from 1981 to 2011. So I really think, for those of us, all of us, who were stunned with the popular uprising, and if you call it a popular uprising, you are showing some kind of bias. If you call it a coup, you are showing another kind.

But whatever you call it, it cannot be, when you think about the fact that here is a people for 30 years had a military dictatorship and no rights, they are struggling to figure it out.

So I want you to help me figure it out, bringing all of your thoughts to the table, and your biases, as we all have them in some way or another. We try not to, but we might.

So what I took from all of this is that there was an absolute fear on the part of, let us say, a majority of the people there, slim or larger, that Morsi was not living up to his commitment to be inclusive.

And that is why, Dr. Dunne, when you explained that this temporary government is including Islamists, as well as secularists, I think that is what you said, although not necessarily the Brotherhood, they are reaching out, I mean isn't that the point? What he promised was everyone would be brought in.

So my sense of it is this absolute fear that Egypt was moving in a direction that was very dangerous, and that if something was not done, they would lose their chance at true democracy.

Now, am I conflating things? Am I being too simplistic?

But I would like to know, if you were to analyze why it happened, how would you explain why this happened after an election?

And I will start with Dennis.

Ambassador Ross. I would say there are several reasons. A, I think there was a perception that many of the people who voted for Morsi felt betrayed. They had expected that there was going to be inclusiveness and there was not. I think there is also, when all segments of society, I think, were involved, it was also looking at what was the near collapse of the Egyptian economy. Life was getting dramatically worse on a daily basis, and there was a perception that this was literally a leadership that was not only incompetent, but it almost seemed indifferent.

So what you had is a perception of a leadership that was authoritarian, exclusive, intolerant, and incompetent.

And it basically produced what I think was this very broad alienation across different segments of the societies. So I think there were multiple factors, but I think it sort of added up to that.

Senator Boxer. Dr. Dunne.

Dr. Dunne. Senator, first of all, I do agree with you about our aid being leverage. And a couple times, the gulf aid has come up as though, well, this can just replace our aid if we withdraw it. The military assistance that the United States has extended, it really means something beyond dollars only. So it is a kind of a relationship, the transfer of technology. It is joint training and exercises, and all these things.

Money deposited in the central bank from gulf donors cannot replace those things.

So there are ways in which it is not only our aid that is leverage, it is our relationship.

Senator BOXER. I appreciate that. That is different from what I thought you said before.

But if you could now move to my question, Why do you think this happened? You called it a coup, so tell us why you think this happened.

Dr. DUNNE. Well, I agree with what you said, that many Egyptians felt that if something was not done, they would lose their chance at democracy.

My concern is about what it was that was done. The petition that was circulated, these enormous demonstrations, were asking for an early Presidential election. That is not what they got.

And my concern is that what was done, the removal of Morsi by coup, and so forth, has damaging implications. And I think we are seeing them right now in the streets of Egypt.

So that is my concern.

Senator BOXER. Do you have anything to add to that?

Ambassador KURTZER. Yes, Senator.

I think if you look at the actual voting patterns that brought Morsi to office, you would see that his support was much broader than just Islamists. And, therefore, as you suggested in your question, there was an expectation that he was going to reach out beyond his own constituency, so he certainly failed these additional voters who had decided on him, as opposed to the former general, Ahmed Shafik.

Senator BOXER. Okay, I have one last question, because my time is running out. I appreciate it so much.

I want to talk about Syria, have you talk about Syria. We know that Morsi was very, very strong, had a strong relationship with the rebel forces, at least part of them. And they were very committed. They took a lot of refugees.

What do you think is going to happen now, in terms of the relationship in that terribly tragic situation in Syria?

We will start with Dennis.

Ambassador ROSS. Well, I do think it is complicated now, from an Egyptian standpoint. I think Morsi was perceived as, in a sense, supporting the call for jihadis to go to Syria. I think that there was a big fear that suddenly you would have these guys go to Syria, then they would come back, and you would re-create a little bit of what happened in Afghanistan and what happened when those people came back to the countries that they had left. So I think that drove some of that.

I think there is probably somewhat of a retrenchment right now in terms of Egyptian attitudes. I do think what the chairman was saying is legitimate, that we really do not want to see them stop being a place where people who are fleeing should be able to come.

So I think this is one of the issues that we should be prepared to emphasize in dealing with this Egyptians.

Dr. DUNNE. Egyptian policy toward Syria is in flux right now. It is rather unclear.

There is a certain tendency to do the opposite of whatever it was that Morsi did. And we have seen this backlash against Syrians inside of Egypt.

At the same time, though, I think the fact that the new Egyptian Government is going to want to have a close relationship with

Saudi Arabia and the UAE and Kuwait will mean that they will want to be within that Arab consensus, which still is that President al-Assad should go.

Ambassador KURTZER. I think what we are going to see, actually, is a revival of what has been a dormant Egyptian diplomacy.

You now have a very strong Foreign Minister in place, Nabil Fahmy, whom many of you know quite well. And Egypt has always believed that it is a diplomatic leader in this region. So you have had Arab policies toward Syria, but you have not had a concerted effort to align those policies.

And I think you may now see an Egypt that tries to strike a leadership role in defining what the Arabs can do to effect change in Syria.

Senator BOXER. Thank you.

The CHAIRMAN. Thank you.

Senator Rubio.

Senator RUBIO. Thank you, Mr. Chairman, and the ranking member, for holding this hearing.

First, let us kind of define what our goal here is with Egyptian policy. I think in two of the written statements here today, it really does a good job of crystallizing it.

Ambassador Ross, you state, certainly, we would like to see Egypt proceed on a path that promotes a representative, inclusive, tolerant government that tackles its problems and respects minority and women's rights, and fulfills its international obligations, including its peace treaty with Israel.

And, Dr. Dunne, you also stated that Egypt can only be a reliable security partner for the United States and a peace partner for Israel if it is reasonably stable, and it will only become stable once it develops a governing system that answers strong popular demands for responsiveness, accountability, fairness, and respect for citizens' rights.

I thought that was very well-stated, and it gives us our goal for what our policy should be.

So what we are trying to figure out is what can United States policy be that moves Egypt in this direction.

I think you would all agree that it is impossible to have that kind of Egypt, unless the rights of everyone are respected, including, for example, the rights—and I will use this for an example because I think it is particularly acute—of the 10 percent of the population which are Coptic Christians. And there is a real challenge in that regard.

The Egyptian Initiative for Personal Rights has stated recently that the post-Morsi security apparatus, which are the folks that are now in charge, have acted slowly and not performed their legally mandated role, failing to intervene to protect citizens, meaning Christian citizens, and their property, despite prior knowledge of these attacks, and even the presence on the scene during some of these attacks.

I think this has become especially problematic in the aftermath, as many Muslim Brotherhood elements are looking to scapegoat Christians as the cause for Morsi's fall.

Amnesty International reports that on July 5, there was an attack that killed four Christians and injured four more as a mob in Luxor attacked these Christian homes and businesses with knives, tree branches, hammers, and metal bars, while security forces stood by and watched.

The situation has gotten so acute that the Coptic Pope, Tawadros II, has now for three straight weeks canceled his weekly afternoon public prayer in Cairo's Cathedral, for fear that the large gathering of Christians would be an easy target for attackers.

So my first question is, in your opinion, as these attacks are happening, and we are getting these reports of the security apparatus not doing anything about it, is this an unwillingness on their part to do anything about it? Is this their inability, because they are not properly trained and equipped to anything about it?

Why are we hearing these reports that they are not doing anything about it?

By the way, there are instances of this happening after Mubarak but before for Morsi as well. Why are they not doing anything about it? Because they cannot, or because they will not?

Ambassador ROSS. I have a suspicion that it is a little bit of both. I think there is a question of capability. I think there is a question of priority. I think there is a question of which battles do they want to fight.

I think all these things are probably coming into play right now. But I do think this is one of those areas of acute concern for us, where I would like us to be able to retain some influence to try to affect their behavior.

Senator RUBIO. Everyone—go ahead.

Dr. DUNNE. Senator Rubio, there has been a long history in Egypt of attacks on Christians, and so forth. And there has been a tendency to sweep them under the rug, to just try to quiet down the communities after these things happen and not to really bring people to justice.

Senator RUBIO. This was during Mubarak as well?

Dr. DUNNE. This was, unfortunately, during Mubarak, during the rule of the SCAF, during the time of Morsi, and now. What is the common thread? An unreformed security sector is what we are seeing, a security sector that really does not take the rule of law seriously at all, and basically makes its decisions on a political basis.

Senator RUBIO. Well, let me tell you why I raise this, beyond the morals aspects of it, because I do agree that we need to be engaged and that our foreign aid programs for all nations, as Senator Boxer pointed out, not just to Egypt, should further our national interests. It is in our national interest that Egypt be stable.

I think we all agree that Egypt cannot be stable if 10 percent of the population feels not just underrepresented in the political branches, but unsafe and that the security apparatus does not protect them.

And so with that in mind, I think this, and insisting on this, should be a critical part of aid moving forward in terms of our insistence that our aid goes toward this, and that, in fact, they respect these rights.

And that is why I question, for example, the need for more F–16s, because I am not sure what F–16s could do against a mob armed with tree branches and hammers.

And beyond that, I would argue that I think we would all agree, and maybe you could elaborate more on this, that until this issue is resolved, until 10 percent of the population that, by the way, has a lot of historical presence in Egypt and is a significant part of Egyptian society, until the 10 percent of Christians and other religious and minority groups and women, and everyone else in Egypt, feel like they truly have a voice in government, but are also safe and able to prosper economically and individually, that you are not going to have the kind of stable Egyptian state that we desperately want, not just for the security of the region but the peace treaty with Israel, et cetera.

Should not our foreign aid, with countries like Egypt and others, be not just geared toward giving them this capacity, but conditioned upon them taking significant steps to ensure that issues that undermine their stability are addressed?

Ambassador KURTZER. Senator, I agree with you fully that the issues that you enumerated in your opening remarks are critical interests of the United States. But there are additional critical interests, which also have to be taken into account: the intelligence relationship, the military relationship, the counterterrorism relationship, Egypt's treaty with Israel as a foundation and cornerstone for everything else we try to do in the peace process.

And that is where the difficulty becomes. We have tried for many years. I spent many hours with President Mubarak, arguing about the need to find a way to deal with these sectarian issues. Some of them have to do with local problems. Some of them have to do with larger historical problems. But the reality was that that regime and the current regime, and the previous regime to the current regime, have not done enough in this regard.

And I think our dialogue with Egypt, and the hopes that we express for where Egypt goes, has to include that.

I am only concerned about the conditionality of conditioning our aid on an important issue, but on only one issue of a very——

Senator RUBIO. And I am not claiming that it should.

I apologize. Obviously, my time is limited, so I can only focus on different aspects. I imagine other members will focus on others.

Clearly, their agreement with Israel is important. Clearly, their counterterrorism cooperation is important, as far as conditionality as well.

But I am just saying that one of the conditions that should be in place in foreign aid with Egypt should include them taking real, measurable steps to protect religious minorities, in particular Christians. And not just that, but the aid we give them should be aid that builds that capacity.

And I am worried that a lot of our aid is geared toward military capacities that they quite frankly do not need. As far as I know, I am not sure that Egypt is in threat of being invaded by any of their neighbors. Hence, the question of why we need to continue to send them fighter jets instead of capacity-building that they could use, so that they do not have to stand by and watch Christians be beat up with hammers and metal bars, or anybody, for that matter. That was my point.

But I do not mean to suggest that that is the only condition. But I do believe it is a significant one, and I am not sure anyone disagrees with that assessment.

The CHAIRMAN. Thank you.

Senator Cardin.

Senator CARDIN. Mr. Chairman, ranking member, thank you very much for this hearing. It is critically important that our committee be engaged as the circumstances are unfolding in Egypt.

As a Senator from Maryland, we have a personal involvement here. As I am sure the committee is aware, the end of June, Andrew Pochter, a 21-year-old college student from Chevy Chase, MD, who was in Egypt to teach English in Alexandria to Egyptian youth, was killed during a protest. So we have felt it personally in our State.

Ambassador Ross, you got my attention when you used the word ''prolonged.'' This could test our patience as we continue to observe changes in Egypt.

I want to talk about our policies in Egypt as to how it affects the region. We have talked about United States aid from the point of view of our influence in bringing about changes within Egypt. I am concerned also about what impact it has on the region.

United States aid to Egypt was basically part of the peace accords reached between Egypt and Israel. The peace agreements between Israel and Jordan, although solid, the circumstances in Syria have raised questions about the stability of Jordan. And we have all seen the on-again, off-again negotiations between the Israelis and the Palestinians, and there has been little hope of progress being made in that direction.

Iran has sort of been off the front pages but obviously that is an area of major concern of stability in the Middle East.

So I would like to get your assessment as to how our involvement in Egypt, particularly as it relates to the foreign aid issue, but just generally, could affect the region, if we were to jeopardize the flow of funds, would it weaken the commitment or the ability to argue for the adherence to the peace agreement with Israel? Would that be more in jeopardy or not? And how does it affect the region?

Ambassador ROSS. It is easy to say that, in the end, the Egyptian military has its own interests and should have its own interests in preserving the peace agreement with Israel. I think at one level, that is true.

But I think we should not underestimate the kind of impulse that if we were to cut the assistance at this point, the kind of impulse it would create among the military to sort of demonstrate the costs to us of having done that.

And I worry about what its implications would be for that treaty. I worry about the implications would be for the behavior in the Sinai, notwithstanding the fact that these still reflect what Egypt's own interests should dictate.

And I think if you look at the potential consequences and you think that those are high and sufficiently adverse, then you have to weigh whether you think it is worth taking that kind of step at that point this point.

I do not think it is worth taking that kind of step at this point, because I think it reduces our influence to the point where I think that we will regret that. And I do not want to put us in that position.

I think it has not only impact within Egypt. But I think it has potential relationship toward what is going on in Sinai, which, by the way, will end up affecting not only the Israelis, but Egypt and maybe elsewhere in the region.

If the Sinai becomes a regional focal point for jihadis, we are going to find that this becomes a threat that radiates outward.

So, from my standpoint, I think it does have a larger consequence within the region.

Senator CARDIN. Dr. Dunne, I listened very carefully to your point. The popular sentiment in Egypt has never been pro-Israel, so if the United States were to take steps that would challenge the Egyptians from the point of view of their independence, does that not put at greater risk the relationship between Israel and Egypt?

Dr. DUNNE. Senator, the Egyptian military and the rest of the Egyptian leadership make these decisions about Israel and about the peace treaty, and so forth, based on their own calculations.

Ambassador Ross was talking a few minutes ago about the issue of the tunnels at Rafah and how the Egyptian military now is upset about Hamas because of things they think Hamas is doing inside of Egypt, and, therefore, they are cutting the tunnels to punish Hamas.

Is not closing those tunnels something the United States has been asking them to do for a long time? So it is when——

Senator CARDIN. I do not challenge that the Egyptians, particularly the military, will make assessments based upon their own interests. That is understandable. My point is the popular sentiment within Egypt.

Dr. DUNNE. And the popular sentiment within Egypt regarding Israel, I mean the positive side of this is that Egyptians have been so preoccupied with their own affairs that we have seen a bit less of the anti-Israel kind of grandstanding that we have seen in Egypt on and off over the years.

I think that is largely reactive to things that happen.

Senator CARDIN. The challenge is that the Egyptians perceive Israel as being a very close friend of the United States, the United States very interested in Israel. The United States takes action, which is not perceived as friendly toward Egypt by cutting off aid or conditioning aid or suspending aid.

Is it not logical that at risk could be the relationship between Israel and Egypt?

Dr. DUNNE. I certainly do not expect Egypt to take any actual aggressive action against Israel because of this.

In terms of the popular sentiment issue, again, it will depend on how the Egyptian military would decide to play this. If there were a suspension of aid, and the Egyptian military, and there was still hope that we would resume this aid as soon as we see——

Senator CARDIN. Let me give Mr. Kurtzer the last 15 seconds.

Ambassador KURTZER. I would offer two brief comments.

Number one, in large policy terms, the constancy of the United States-Egyptian relationship is critically important to our interests elsewhere in the region. If we are seen as walking away easily from this longstanding relationship, it will impact what we do else-where.

Number two, it is critically important that we support Egypt as a cornerstone of the Egyptian-Israeli peace treaty. And the best proof of this are the newspaper stories this week that have sug-gested that Israel has been lobbying our administration not to cut aid to Egypt, because Israel understands that that would be against its interests with respect to respecting the peace treaty.

Senator CARDIN. Thank you, Mr. Chairman.

The CHAIRMAN. Thank you.

Senator Johnson.

Senator JOHNSON. Thank you, Mr. Chairman, for holding the hearing.

And thank you for your thoughtful testimony and answers to the questions.

I would like to understand a little bit more about the current political profile of the population.

Dr. Dunne, you had an interesting comment in your testimony, saying that the current alliance certainly is anti-Muslim Brother-hood, but not necessarily anti-Islamist. Can you further explain that comment?

Dr. DUNNE. Senator, I said that because I think there is a danger of ours—in the United States—seeing what is happening in Egypt in a way that we would like to see it, that we would like to see secularism as opposed to Islamism.

But there is an Islamist partner, the Salafi al-Nour party, which is more ideologically extreme than the Muslim Brotherhood and which is working with the military and the transition government, and so forth. So we will continue to see Islamist language in the constitution, and all of that.

In terms of the affiliation of the population, probably the best thing to do is to look at the several sets of elections that have been held in Egypt, and where the voting has gone.

In the past, the voting has indicated that there is somewhere between 40 to 70 percent of the population that will tend to vote Islamist. It has varied a little bit from election to election.

Now that might go down now with the political fortunes of the Brotherhood falling, but Islamists are going to continue to be a big part of Egyptian society and a big part of the political spectrum.

Senator JOHNSON. Ambassador Kurtzer, you refer to the popu-lation as evenly divided. Can you describe that even division? Divided between what?

Ambassador KURTZER. Well, we saw in the election of the Presi-dency when Morsi was elected that he won with about 51-point-something percent, which suggested that 49-point-something per-cent was on the other side.

Now it was a bit of an artificial divide because you had polar-izing candidates. You had an Islamist candidate on the one hand, and you had a candidate very associated with the Mubarak regime on the other. And all of those who had stood in the first round of the election, who might be called more centrist, had not made the cut.

So you do not have a good test case yet to know how an election would play itself out, were you to have a better choice.

Senator JOHNSON. Again, I am trying to get a description. Is it Islamists versus pro-democracy versus pro-stability? Can you give me some sort of feel in terms of what is the population feeling? What are they leaning toward?

Ambassador KURTZER. Well, number one, I would point to the fact that there is broad national support for the Egyptian military. It does not necessarily translate into electoral support unless they put forward a candidate, which they are unlikely to do.

Senator JOHNSON. Well, that would be pro-stability, then basically.

Ambassador KURTZER. Pro-stability.

Senator JOHNSON. Okay.

Ambassador KURTZER. You have, as Dr. Dunne indicated, you have from election results for Parliament, Shura Council, and the Presidency, we assume that there is 35 percent to 40 percent of the population that will vote Islamist, either for the Brotherhood or for the more fundamentalist Salafist al-Nour Party. So you have that kind of a breakdown.

You have a large population that is undefined that is able to bring people out on the street to indicate what they do not want, but they have not yet coalesced around a political philosophy. These are the folks who brought about this many million person protest movement.

But they then break down. There are some nationalists and socialists. There are some liberals. There are all kinds of strains between.

There is something called the National Salvation Front, which has sought to become an umbrella for these groups, but it has not yet represented a coherent alternative policy.

Senator JOHNSON. I do want to talk a little bit about foreign aid, but just quickly, in terms of their economy, how much of their economy is really driven by tourism? What percent? In the good days?

Ambassador KURTZER. Oh, in the good days, the rent part of the economy, tourism, Suez Canal, expatriate workers, represented upward of, I would guess, 70 percent to 80 percent of their foreign exchange income. In other words, a huge amount of the Egyptian——

Senator JOHNSON. So without stability, Egypt's economy is going to be a basket case.

Ambassador KURTZER. Oh, for sure. When I arrived in Egypt as Ambassador in 1998, it was right after a major terrorist attack. There was no tourism and they were suffering at that point, even though the economy otherwise was in reasonable shape.

Senator JOHNSON. So the rational thing for the population would be pro-stability?

Ambassador KURTZER. Yes.

Senator JOHNSON. Let me talk a little bit about foreign aid, because it is extremely complex. It is incredibly unpopular here in the United States, obviously.

Ambassador Kurtzer, you talked about, we need to be careful because we have to be quiet in some of our dealings with Egypt.

But at the same time, before going to continue foreign aid, we are going to have to be somewhat public about attaching conditions, attaching some controls. I mean, how do you deal with that very delicate balance if foreign aid is going to continue so we can maintain the type of influence that I think most of us would like to be able to provide, so we can provide that stability?

Ambassador KURTZER. Well, the quiet dialogue that has to take place all the time presumably would lead to some degree of understanding as to why conditionality or a set of goals are attached to our legislation.

I think pronouncements that come out in the midst of deliberations, whether they be from the administration or in Congress, have a tendency to get magnified when they are reported in Egypt. And it does not give our administration representatives, or even congressional delegations, the chance to have these quiet conversations.

I am sure all of you, as you have visited Egypt, have had the opportunity to have these quite discussions, and they actually can work sometimes, rather than pronouncements coming out of the State Department spokesman or the White House spokesman.

Senator JOHNSON. Senator Cardin was talking about the requirement of foreign aid attached to the Camp David Accords. When did that the obligation of the United States run out?

Ambassador KURTZER. Senator, it is not obligation per se. It is voted upon regularly by the Congress. It was an undertaking to support the peace treaty back in 1979, and it has been renewed ever since, to the tune of upward of $70 billion of American assistance, both economic and military. But there is no long-term commitment that has been written into legislation.

Senator JOHNSON. Okay, thank you, Mr. Chairman.

The CHAIRMAN. Thank you.

Senator Shaheen.

Senator SHAHEEN. Thank you, Mr. Chairman.

Thank you to our panelists for being here today.

As we observe how Egypt goes forward, what are the risks to the transition if the Muslim Brotherhood is totally excluded from any future coalition that forms to run the government?

And I do not know who would like to address that?

Ambassador Ross.

Ambassador ROSS. I think the key point to understand is they represent an important social force within Egypt. So if you exclude what is an important social force within Egypt, then this is basically a prescription for trouble, because they are going to express themselves some way.

What we have right now is a reaction to the ouster of President Morsi. The question is whether or not there can be some vehicle for bringing those who are part of the Muslim Brotherhood back into the political process.

What I was saying in my testimony is they should not be excluded. If they choose to take themselves out of the equation, that is one thing. But they should not be excluded.

And I do not believe it is going to be easy to bring them back in right now, simply because I think they are so determined to make a statement that, for the time being, it is going to be difficult.

I do not assume that will remain the case forever, because not only are they a social force, but they have their own interests in being represented, they have their own interests in trying to influence what is going to happen in Egypt.

Senator SHAHEEN. And to what extent does it seem like there is an understanding or willingness to bring them in? Do we think that that is something the military, the current civilian folks in charge, appreciate or are willing to support?

Ambassador ROSS. I will just say——

Senator SHAHEEN. Would you respond and then Dr. Dunne?

Ambassador ROSS. I will just say the words we are hearing are the right words. The question is whether the behavior reflects the words.

Senator SHAHEEN. Dr. Dunne.

Dr. DUNNE. Senator Shaheen, Egypt just went through a period from December 2012 until now where there was a constitution passed and laws and so forth, and elections being prepared, from which a significant part of the body politic, in that case, the secularists, felt excluded, objected to, and it led to everything that we saw happen just now.

So I think that if the Brotherhood, which is a very significant movement in Egypt, is excluded this time around, we are going to be headed for more of this. We are going to be headed for a cycle of instability. So there is that.

Regarding the sincerity of including the Brotherhood now, I think the desire is to cut the Brotherhood down to size through arresting their leadership and so forth, and maybe to include them in some very disadvantaged condition. And they are not agreeing to that, of course.

Ambassador Kurtzer mentioned earlier that there may be negotiations going on, whether among Egyptians, or perhaps with some European mediation, that could bring about some sort of agreement on this.

But it is going to be difficult. It is very difficult for the Brotherhood to swallow this, that they elected this President, and he is removed in this way. And unfortunately, the way he was removed allows them to escape from how badly they failed in leadership.

Ambassador KURTZER. Senator, I would like to sharpen the point that Dennis indicated on social cohesion as a problem, as a risk.

I think the risk is actually much more severe if, in fact, a national reconciliation cannot take place. What do I mean by that? The Brotherhood has a long history, 85 years, most of which time living underground and operating outside the system, developing a very significant infrastructure outside the purview of the state.

Right now, today, they have adopted tactics that are confronting the authorities, and they have decided that that is the best way to build up the support that they used to have. If they decide not to engage in a national reconciliation process that is real—in other words, if the process is real or the offer is real and they decide not to, they could also decide to engage in what we would call an insurgency.

And they would have that capability, not just because of their underground history, but also because this is a region where weapons are easy to come by, and where jihadists are easy to come by. They cross borders at will.

So I do not want to sound alarmist, but this is not simply a question of the lack of social cohesion. This could deteriorate and it could deteriorate rapidly, if, A, the offer for reconciliation is not real, or, B, if it is real and the Brotherhood says ''No'' to it.

Senator SHAHEEN. One of the things that got a lot of attention here at the outset of the revolution in Egypt was when the Morsi government proposed a law to require the national security committee to approve all NGO activities. Obviously, people remembered the representatives from IRI and NDI who were jailed and how they were treated.

And it seems to me, as we think about how can we support countries like Egypt, that one of the sectors that is really critical is the civil society sector. So do we have any sense of what this interim government is going to do with respect to NGOs and civil society leaders? And is there more that we should be doing or could be doing to try and support those civil society leaders?

Ambassador ROSS. The short answer; we do not know yet. But this is one of those areas that would be the best indication that they are for real about wanting to create a genuine political process that changes the future of Egypt, that creates in Egypt a representative, inclusive, tolerant society where there is genuine political space for real political pluralism.

The key to that is going to be building civil society institutions. The willingness to embrace and rewrite the laws, to pardon those who are prosecuted and found guilty, I think that becomes a very significant measure of the direction of Egypt, and it should be a focal point of where we try to use their leverage.

Senator SHAHEEN. Dr. Dunne.

Dr. DUNNE. I agree with Ambassador Ross about that. I think the treatment of civil society, freedom for civil society and for the media, will be some of the leading indicators of where things are going, and that it is something we should press on.

One thing we have to remember is that our problem about this with civil society—and this is why the United States is not giving any civil society to Egypt, has not been for some time now, because of the NGO case that you mentioned, Senator.

This started under military rule. So it was not a problem under Morsi. It was a problem under both, both under the SCAF and under Morsi. So this is something that one would hope could be corrected now.

Senator SHAHEEN. Thank you.

Ambassador KURTZER. Senator, having been the harbinger of gloom on the previous question, let me be a little more optimistic here.

If you look at the composition of this interim government, they are actually quite good people, many graduates of the American University in Cairo, people who grew up with a more liberal education.

So, yes, the past has been a real problem and it has been a very significant challenge for us. But I think it is something to build on, because I think we may have a government in place that actually understands the importance of civil society.

The CHAIRMAN. Thank you.

Senator Flake.

Senator FLAKE. I will yield my time to Senator McCain.

The CHAIRMAN. Senator McCain.

Senator McCAIN. Thank you, Mr. Chairman.

The CHAIRMAN. It is that Arizona collegiality.

Senator McCAIN. Not to take away from my time, but we believe in the early-bird rule. I guess it is not where you stand; it is where you sit.

Mr. Chairman, I thank you.

I thank the witnesses. I want to discuss for a minute the issue of the one thing that the United States of America stands for is the rule of law, which clearly Morsi ignored and perverted and took powers onto himself, which were not in keeping with his own constitution.

So we have a law, and that law states very clearly, without a national security waiver, as most laws that we pass do, it says a coup or a decree will occasion a cutoff of aid to whatever country there is.

So now I see my friends here say, ''Well, he was a bad guy. Well, the people supported it overwhelmingly. It was very popular to have this coup.'' And as Dr. Dunne pointed out, there were elections scheduled fairly soon.

So we are now in a situation, much to my regret, where we are asking the new government to write a constitution, have laws, and respect and abide by those rules of law. But for purposes of practicality, or whatever reason we might use, we are not going to cut off at aid.

And I do not see a coherent policy toward Egypt. I note this morning we are not going to deliver F–16s. We are not cutting off aid, but were not going to deliver F–16s.

I do not see a coherent policy toward Egypt. And if I were those people in the street in Cairo, I would not understand it either.

There is a risk of us enforcing our laws that we could alienate some people in Egypt who would think we are siding with the Muslim Brotherhood. The general, El-Sisi, has now called for demonstrations, demonstrations in the street to support what they are doing against Morsi. And we see violence taking place in various parts of Egypt, and threats of more.

The one thing I think the Muslim Brotherhood knows how to do, and that is operate underground. They did it for many, many years, and they are pretty good at it.

And it was a very tough call for me and Senator Graham to make the decisions that we made, but I am not sure how we ask another country to impose rule of law and abide by it, and we do not for purposes that we think are more important, or whatever.

And by the way, I am glad we are writing a new law which does condition aid I think very appropriately. But the present law is on the books.

So I guess my question to you, Ambassador Ross, who I admire enormously, how do we reconcile that? What do you think about the suspension of the F–16s? Do we have a policy, a coherent policy that Members of Congress and the American people and the Egyptian people can understand?

If I could have those responses from all three witnesses?

Ambassador ROSS. Look, the issues you raise, the principles you talk about, I understand and I respect. And I think it is a terrible dilemma. It is a very difficult dilemma.

The only reason that I do not favor the cutoff of assistance is not because I do not respect the principle; it is that I worry about what the consequence is going to be if we do it at this point.

I believe that, in fact, we should retain the ability to cut it off at some point, if there is not responsiveness to us. But I am afraid if we do it right now, the effect is going to be that we lose the key connection we have with the one institution in Egypt that I think has some potential for restoring stability, which is the military. I think we lose a very significant part of the Egyptian public who are going to read this as having been an American dictate against the popular will. And I am afraid that our capacity to influence the military to do things in a direction that gives us a chance to establish the kind of rule of law we would like to see take place——

Senator MCCAIN. And the F–16s?

Ambassador ROSS. The F–16, the way I read it is that the administration is sending a signal that there is a limit to their patience, that they want the military to understand that they mean what they say, that if there is not a responsiveness to us at some point, that we will act on the assistance. I see it as a step that is designed to send a signal.

Senator MCCAIN. That was the signal, I thought, by suspending aid, that until certain things happen, it was also a motivation to do so. But I respect your views on it, and I know it is the tough call.

Dr. Dunne.

Dr. DUNNE. Senator, I agree with you. There has not been a coherent policy toward Egypt. And I agree with you on respecting our own law regarding suspending the assistance.

One of the problems the administration faces now is that because they did not stand up for principle when Morsi was there, now they feel they cannot stand up for it now.

It just seems to me as though we are piling mistake upon mistake in our policy toward Egypt. And it really is time to take a breath and to rethink.

I also think that the suspension of aid can be done in a way to indicate that we are not cutting off all relations. We are not cutting off all cooperation. It does not necessarily have to be that way. And it would be the choice of the Egyptian military.

And I would hope that they would choose not to cut off their nose to spite the face, because we are required by our law to suspend the aid temporarily until they come through on their promise to restore democratic process.

Ambassador KURTZER. Senator, I know the lawyers have been jumping through hoops to find a definition of coup that fits one definition or the other. And I will not get into that.

Senator MCCAIN. It takes a pretty adept lawyer to contradict that language, but I understand.

Ambassador KURTZER. If it looks like a coup and walks like a coup, I will not take it from there.

But I will say the following, as I mentioned earlier, this is a very young revolution, and the Egyptian system has gotten it wrong twice, both with the SCAF, the Supreme Council of the Armed Forces, as the interim government, and then Morsi as an elected bad government.

Morsi did things that were against the rule of law, contrary to what we would call the democratic process.

The question then is whether a move that we do believe is contrary to the rule of law—i.e., the military intervening—can actually be the dynamic that pushes Egypt or gives Egypt a chance to get it right this third time.

Now that does not answer the legal question, but it does, in a sense, underscore the policy dilemma that we are all facing.

Senator McCain. And the F–16s?

Ambassador Kurtzer. I do not understand the F–16s, other than as an immediate reaction to what General El-Sisi said yesterday. And if that is the case, you know, I am not sure it makes any sense to have done it.

If there was a justification for the F–16 sale to Egypt, that justification should stand anyway, and I assume that the F–16s will be delivered at some point.

Senator McCain. Thank you, Mr. Chairman.

And I thank my friend from Arizona.

The Chairman. Thank you, Senator McCain.

Senator Kaine.

Senator Kaine. Thank you, Mr. Chair, and to the witnesses, this has been an important hearing and many of my questions have already been addressed. But let me just go to a couple of things.

We need to do what is best in our own assessment of American interests, but I do think perceptions of our allies in the region are important; an important factor for us to consider.

I returned from a codel that was led by Senator Cornyn over the Fourth of July, and we spent time in both Jordan and the UAE. And this was right at the time of the development of the street protests and the fall of the Morsi government.

Both the Jordanians and UAE government officials we met with were strongly in favor of continuing support to the Egyptian military.

And while I have not had direct conversations with Israeli governmental officials, at least what you read in the press, both American and Israeli press, would suggest that they feel the same.

That has been a theme of the testimony this morning, but to just kind of put it in a direct question, would you say that these critical American allies, Jordan, UAE, and Israel, in the neighborhood would be in a strong position that the United States should continue aid to the government and especially the military government as a stabilizing force during this time?

Ambassador Ross. The answer is absolutely ''Yes.'' All of them see Egypt as an essential pillar of stability in the region, and all of them would be profoundly concerned if they saw us taking this step because they would worry about what the reaction would be.

Senator Kaine. Dr. Dunne.

Dr. Dunne. Senator, yes, those allies are in favor of continuing the aid. But I would note that their interests regarding Egypt differ from ours.

Senator Kaine. Absolutely.

Dr. DUNNE. Even my fellow panelists who are against suspension of aid have been raising the democracy, human rights, civil society, free media, rights of all citizens, including Christians. These interests of ours that the United States has, those allies generally do not take an interest in such issues.

Senator KAINE. I would not characterize it as not taking interest in those issues. I think that goes too far. That is my own editorial comment.

And I agree. We have to make the right decision for our interests, but the interests of close allies that we have, who admittedly look at it differently. One of the reasons they look at it differently is they are in the neighborhood, and we are many, many time zones away. The perceptions of our close allies are a factor in trying to reach the right decision in terms of our interests.

Ambassador Kurtzer.

Ambassador KURTZER. The answer to your question is ''Yes.'' I would simply go beyond it to say, look, the challenge we have now is we want to promote democracy; we want to maintain our significant interests; we want to maintain the constancy of our relationship. And sometimes these things are going to come into contradiction with one another.

But there is a fourth element, which goes to the heart of your question, Senator, and I agree with it fully. In some respects, if Egypt gets it right this time, and if we get it right this time, Egypt can be the model for democratic change in the region that people have been talking about for 2 years.

Right now, it is not that model, because it has not yet found its footing. It does not even know where it is heading and how it is going to build this democratic culture, democratic institutions, and so forth.

So, yes, the region is going to look at this carefully. The constancy of our relationship is important. And if we get it right, the payoff regionally, not just in Egypt, is also going to be quite important.

Senator KAINE. On this discussion about trying to get it right, I want to pursue some questions that Senator Johnson was raising earlier, trying to have a better understanding of the character of the internal political dynamic. One of the things that was so obvious and inspiring about the initial protests that toppled the previous government was the significant participation of young people and a significant number of what I would think of, what I would characterize as, sort of secular oppositionists. So much of the discussion that we have had today in the media is about the military and the Muslim Brotherhood.

Dr. Dunne has pointed out that there are Islamists to the right of the Muslim Brotherhood. I guess I do not know if you call it right or left. More Islamic than the Muslim Brotherhood.

But what about the youth movement and secular opposition movement? Is that still vibrant? Have they been as active in recent protests as they were in the original protests in Tahrir Square? Talk to us a little bit about that segment of society, which I gathered from all your answers is somewhat unorganized. They have not been able to unify under a particular banner. But knowing the strength of their passions and their numbers might tell us something important as well.

Ambassador ROSS. Well, they have not gone away. In fact, I think they were the key to the movement, the rebellion movement, the organization of the petitions. This was done, again, by a very small number of young people who focused on what was their recourse.

When someone refers to this as being a popular uprising, it was because there was a perception there was not an alternative out there. There was not any other option.

There still is the problem that there is not the kind of coherence to this. There is not an unmistakable political platform. There is not an unmistakable political agenda. There is not an organization that is geared toward having a political program.

And that is one of the things that is so critical. It is one of the reasons I think some of us put the focus on building civil society organizations and allowing NGOs to function, precisely so that you can take what is this impulse that knows what it does not want and begin to channel it into something much more constructive in terms of what they do want.

Dr. DUNNE. Yes, Senator, I think the secular part of the political spectrum really has been revitalized in the last few months, even well before June 30. They were looking toward parliamentary elections before that, and they realized that they had to do a much better job than they have done in the past in organizing politically, in order to compete with the Brotherhood primarily and the Salafis. So that was already happening.

I do not know if there is ever going to be any single secular political party. There probably is not, because there really are differences among them. There are liberals. There are leftists. There are revolutionaries. And they are not necessarily all going to be able to come together in one political force. But they certainly could coalesce into two or three more viable parties.

There is a difference among them right now regarding the Brotherhood. There are those within the secular opposition who say the Brotherhood has to be included somehow or we are in for trouble. And there are others who are just happy to see their rivals decimated, however it happens, and hope to reap political advantage during the next elections because of that.

Ambassador KURTZER. Senator, we have been lamenting during this hearing the absence of civil society. I would say it is just the opposite. What we have seen for 2 years is the face of the Egyptian civil society, and it is very exciting. You have millions of people ready to participate in politics and to try to effect change.

Now, as we all know, they do not have a positive agenda yet. They are not well-organized. They are not quite coherent with respect to what they want proactively.

But the raw material for building that civil society is now manifest. We now know what it looks like.

I would also add that even within the Muslim Brotherhood, there is more pluralism than is suggested in what we see in the press. When you read Muslim Brotherhood Web sites, there is debate going on between the older generation and the younger generation, between those who want to open up the movement more and those who want to keep it the way it was.

So there are a lot of these things going on in this laboratory of change, which makes this a very exciting time in Egypt.

Senator KAINE. Thank you, Mr. Chairman.

The CHAIRMAN. Thank you.

Senator Paul.

Senator PAUL. I want to thank the panel for coming today, and expressing your opinions.

I would like to know a fairly direct response on whether or not you think the military takeover in Egypt was a coup or not a coup.

Ambassador ROSS. A legal definition, I would say it is pretty hard to say it is not a coup.

Senator PAUL. Okay.

Dr. DUNNE. Yes, Senator, I believe it was coup. It had a lot of popular support, but that is often the case with military coups. That is not unique to this case.

Ambassador KURTZER. Well, just so we have one point of difference, I would hesitate to call it a coup, because the military has not taken power. They continue to stand behind the seat of power, but they have made it clear through the roadmap that they issued and their actions since then that they want to see the restoration of the civilian government.

Senator PAUL. Well, the reason that this is important is because our law says that when a coup occurs, the aid ends. So we can debate whether it is good idea to end, and you are welcome to have opinions on whether it is good idea to have aid or not to have aid, but the law is the law. And if we decide that we are above the law, it is very hard for us to be preaching to the rest of the world about having the rule of law.

So I think this seriously undermines our standing in the world, and it seriously goes against anyone who claims that they are for the rule of law.

But I would go one step further. Even if you say this is not a coup because there is not a general currently running it, I think that is semantics, and really not going to the point of this, because our law says, basically, if the military had a substantial involvement in replacing a democratically elected government, so it does not matter, according to our law, whether there is a general in charge or not.

But putting a President who has been elected under house arrest, we do not know where some of these people are. I mean, this is the definition of the kind of thing that we are supposedly opposed to.

And I was no great fan of the Muslim Brotherhood. I was not for aiding the Muslim Brotherhood, either. But the thing is, if we are not going to obey the law, if we are simply going to say that we bring a panel before us that says aid is a good idea, realize that if you are telling us that the aid should continue, you are telling us to flout the law. You are telling us that the law is not important, and that basically we can decide the benefits or the detriments of whether or not to continue aid are more important than the law.

And to my mind, if you are, you are rising to a level where you say you are above everything we stand for. If the President is not going to adhere to the rule of law, if he is going to say he creates the law, we so damage our standing in the world, we so damage what we stand for, that we have no moral basis for going around the world or telling anybody anything.

There is a huge argument we can have about whether it is a good idea or a bad idea. I personally think that if we think we are buying the goodwill of the Egyptian people when they are being doused with tear gas that was made in Pennsylvania, paid for with U.S. taxpayer dollars, I do not think they are jumping up and down and saying "Yay, America."

So I would say that I think foreign aid has often gone to criminals. It has often gone to plutocrats. It has often gone to dictators. It has often gone into the pockets of one plutocrat who then goes and fills up a Louis Vuitton bag full of cash and goes and spends it in Paris. And it is obscene. And I think for us to be defending aid to Egypt when we have given $60 billion of it to the Mubarak family who are basically thieves and stole it, and used it for their own personal aggrandizement—you look at Mobutu and his family. You look at the history of foreign aid. You look at the history of thievery and thuggery, and people who have taken the money and used it for their own personal benefit. And then we are going to come here and say one versus the other?

I truly fear that even out of the military establishment, which everybody says is so much more pro-Western, that what we are going to get out of the military establishment, what we could get, is someone who rises up and becomes a strong man and says, I will correct this chaos in Egypt, and I will do it, but I will do it through the strength of being a general that will do whatever I want. And maybe whatever I want means reclaiming lands that we say Israel has taken from us. Or that maybe someday our weapons are used.

But I think it is absolutely chaos over there, to be sending planes and tanks into this chaos.

But above and beyond all, the debate really is, are we going to obey the law? I do not think really other than some objections, there are serious people out there saying this is not a coup. To define this as not a coup is not to have an intelligent debate, from my point of view.

But I would love to see or hear if there is a justification for breaking the law, because if this is a coup, and you want to continue aid, you are basically arguing for breaking the law.

Ambassador KURTZER. Senator, since I was the one who refused to call it a coup, let me take the first crack at responding. And I would respond to two points you made.

First, on the question of foreign aid, which is a different issue from what we are talking about, perhaps this requires a longer discussion, but I think we can be proud of the billions of dollars of aid that we provide to Egypt, both military and economic. We helped build a country that was largely broken——

Senator PAUL. Including what Mubarak stole.

Ambassador KURTZER. I think it has yet to be determined that Mubarak stole our money.

Senator PAUL. And how would you respond to the fact that El-Sisi, who is from the military, is the Assistant Prime Minister or the Deputy Prime Minister? That to me sounds like the military is involved in the government.

Ambassador KURTZER. That is the second part of the question.

On the first part, I would be happy to discuss further what our aid did accomplish over the years. And it accomplished a great deal.

On the second part of the question, the system that existed under Morsi provided no outlet, no legal outlets, to remove the President, because the court had suspended the people's assembly, their Parliament, which would have been the avenue to pursue a rule of law methodology for removing the President.

And, therefore, when the military did intervene, it was intervening on the basis of what it defined as a popular will. The 10, 15, 20 million people who had not only signed a petition but who had put their address down and their identity card number, who had gone on the streets and who had make clear that they wanted to see a change.

Now, again, and I do not think it is a——

Senator PAUL. You know, hundreds of thousands of people have signed petitions against Obamacare. Do you think if the generals take over the White House and we get rid of Obamacare through force, would that be a coup?

Ambassador KURTZER. Senator, fortunately, we have a system which allows for a rule of law methodology for holding a President accountable. And we have used that in our history.

Egypt during the year of Morsi's governance did not have that methodology. And that is why this is a question mark. I do not think it is a black and white question, frankly.

The CHAIRMAN. Thank you very much.

Senator Markey.

Senator MARKEY. Thank you, Mr. Chairman, very much.

My own view is that the Obama administration is taking carefully calibrated actions to elicit specific, narrow responses in Egypt from all sides. And the F–16 decision is part of that, as is every other part of their strategy. And I think that they are handling a very volatile situation in the best way that they can. And I think we all understand that.

I was in Egypt last March, having left Libya and Tunisia. In each country, they were drafting their constitution. And in each country, there was a Muslim Brotherhood principally responsible in the leadership role for drafting the constitution. And each one of them was clearly trying to draft a constitution that reflected their religious values, but also the history of their country.

And so there is not a one-size-fits-all, in terms of Muslim Brotherhoods, because they are different in each country because they each have a different history.

My question to you is this, as they begin to draft a new constitution, what is it that you would like to see included in this constitution that was not in the last constitution? What is it that you believe could be a consensus amongst those that were protesting that could be agreed upon, that would be included in this constitution? Because I think the words in the constitution are ultimately going to logically determine the outcome, whether or not all parties feel that something fair and something that is reflective of Egypt of today was included in the constitution.

So, do any of you wish to tell me what you would like to see in the constitution, or what you believe the consensus is amongst those who are protesting?

Ambassador Ross. I will make a quick comment. I think the key is going to be the respect for minority rights, and for women's rights, and how that is expressed.

The former constitution had different shadings in it that I think raised questions in both of those areas.

I just make one other quick response to Senator Paul——

Senator MARKEY. If I may, let me just move forward on my question, if I may.

Dr. DUNNE. I would say there are three points to be looking for as to whether this is a constitution being developed that would help create a solid democracy in Egypt.

One of them, certainly, is protection for the rights of all citizens, equal rights for all citizens, lack of discrimination and not different rights in the constitution for different kinds of citizens, women and men, Muslim and non-Muslim, et cetera. So that is one thing to look for.

Another thing that was absent in the constitution that the Brotherhood passed was a rebalancing of powers among the executive, legislative, and judicial branches. The executive has been very powerful in Egypt, and that was something that Egyptians were demanding, that the legislature, in particular, should have more power, and that the independence of the judiciary should be protected.

Senator MARKEY. Are you optimistic that that will be included in the new constitution?

Dr. DUNNE. That is really not clear. You know, it is really not clear. They have a committee to rewrite the constitution. There is not much guidance in terms of what they are going to do.

Senator MARKEY. Ambassador Kurtzer, please.

Ambassador KURTZER. Yes, I would agree with what Dr. Dunne said in both respects and just add one little twist, and that is that the provisions that need to be strengthened with regard to the protection of minorities and women and so forth also have to be balanced off against the way that this new constitution defines Islam as a basis for legislation.

It will say that, but in the previous constitution, it said it in a way that suggested to people that there was going be a long-term process of Islamisation, which I think made people nervous.

Senator MARKEY. So do you think there is a consensus amongst those who were protesting that that is something that has to be clarified, so that there is not kind of an incremental, over time, movement toward that Islamisation?

Ambassador KURTZER. I would think for sure the masses that came out on the streets are unified around this idea. Whether or not they can translate that incoherent political will into the politics of reforming the constitution remains to be seen.

Senator MARKEY. And it could in fact elicit a counterrevolution, if it is included in the constitution? Is that your opinion?

Ambassador KURTZER. Yes. It could.

Senator MARKEY. Do you agree with that, Mr. Ross?

Ambassador ROSS. Yes.

Senator MARKEY. A few days ago, the U.N. High Commissioner for Human Rights announced that it had requested to send a delegation to monitor the situation in Cairo. The Egyptian Government claims it has never received such a request.

Do any of you know what the status is of that request to have a monitoring capacity inside of Cairo, looking at these human rights issues?

How do you see the influence of the neighboring countries? You have Qatar on the one hand, and you have Saudi Arabia and the United Arab Emirates on the other hand. Could you elaborate a little bit on this set of countervailing pressures that exists from the outside on the results that each seeks to achieve?

Ambassador ROSS. Well, there is no doubt that the Saudis, the Emirates, and the Kuwaitis have immediately come in to provide support for the new government, for the interim government, and for what has happened. The fact that they have pledged $12 billion, the fact that they have already begun providing the assistance, they clearly see this as, from their standpoint, a strategic course correction that they want to see cemented. They want the new leadership to look effective.

I think, it is interesting, Qatar had provided a lot of money. And the real question is whether or not there is some rethinking on Qatar's part. I suspect the greatest influence from the region is going to come much more from the Gulf States at this point, meaning the Saudis, the Emirates, and the Kuwaitis.

Senator MARKEY. May I just have a followup, because I have 30 seconds left? Do you think we can solve these human rights problems in Egypt if we do not have the United Nations on site to document what is happening, so that it can be an evidentiary-based discussion that goes on, in terms of who has been harmed, who is being prosecuted, persecuted? Is it necessary, in your opinion, to have the United Nations in, in order to be able to do that work?

Can we just get a quick answer from each of you, please?

Dr. DUNNE. Senator, on this question, I would say there has to be some kind of international engagement, whether it is the United Nations or others. Egypt has been quite resistant to this. They tend to see this as interference in their internal affairs.

But there really is a real danger of escalating human rights abuses in the situation.

On the regional players, I wanted to add, briefly, Turkey is a major player here, and one who I think really has a difference with Saudi Arabia and the others, in terms of whether the removal of Morsi was a good thing.

Senator MARKEY. I just want to get the human rights answer. Do we need the United Nations? I think we do, in order to make sure there is some referee of what is actually happening.

Ambassador KURTZER. Egypt would be well-advised to say yes, in order to dispel any doubts about its behavior. We are able, through our Embassy, our human rights reports, to do what we can. But I think the international legitimacy of the United Nations would help Egypt.

Senator MARKEY. Mr. Ross.

Ambassador ROSS. I agree with that, both on that and also on the issue of elections. You need international observers in there.

Senator MARKEY. Okay, thank you.

Thank you, Mr. Chairman.

The CHAIRMAN. Thank you.

We have a vote, and you have been very resilient here for nearly 2 hours. Just one set of final questions.

One is, it has been—what?—30 years, almost, since the Camp David Accords funded Egypt under Mubarak. That is pretty much the time period, right?

Is what happened to Mubarak a coup?

Ambassador ROSS. We can get into the legal definitions of this, and I am not a lawyer, and maybe I answered more quickly than I should have on this. I think, from my own standpoint, there is a larger set of strategic issues that we have to keep in mind when we evaluate these issues. And that is why I said, from my standpoint, we need to be able to protect the assistance right now.

Dr. DUNNE. Senator, yes; Mubarak was also removed by a coup after a popular uprising. But the difference is that he was not democratically elected.

The CHAIRMAN. Well, my point is, I find it interesting when we pick and choose talking about the rule of law, because if, in fact, Mubarak was a coup, then assistance to Egypt at that time, based upon the view that it was a coup, would have been suspended. And while I understand, Doctor, your comment that he was not democratic, for 30 years, we assisted an undemocratic regime.

So it is a little difficult to split the hairs on that one, when, in fact, you have national security interests that I think are prevailing.

But I just think about when we choose to say that the rule of law should be observed and when not. And so it depends on what your strict definition is, at the end of the day.

Let me ask you this, what could be the offer of reconciliation? We talked about the importance of having an all-inclusive Egypt, and Egypt for all, what could be an offer of reconciliation that would bring the Muslim Brotherhood back as part of an Egypt for all?

Ambassador KURTZER. I think there are two issues that are paramount, and one that is probably not doable.

Number one, there would have to be an end to the arrests and incarceration of those in the Brotherhood who have been arrested since July 3. Those who have really broken the law should stand trial. But in most cases, these have been preventive arrests.

Number two, inclusion of Muslim Brotherhood representatives in the interim government, make room for them in the administration.

The one issue that is probably not doable is the restoration of Mr. Morsi as President, which has been a precondition of the Muslim Brotherhood. So they are going to have to climb down the tree on that issue.

But perhaps the other issues might be incentive enough to enter into a dialogue.

The CHAIRMAN. Any other thoughts on that?

And finally, is it possible to envision an Egypt for all when you have this tension between secularism and Islamists who seem to want—at least Morsi when he was in power—seem to want to have the country move in a direction that is different than what a greater part, obviously, as a result of this uprising of civil society wanted to see? How do you reconcile in the effort to have an Egypt for all with those who want to see embedded in the law elements of a religious point of view and those of the society who want to keep religion as maybe as we consider it in the United States, separate and apart from its government.

How do you reconcile that?

Ambassador KURTZER. Senator, one of the things I did as Ambassador was to invite people involved in our civil rights movement to do lectures in Egypt. And the reason was to help Egyptians understand that you have to start somewhere on the path to real democratic governance, but it may take time and it may take a very hard effort.

So the answer to your question is ''Yes,'' it is possible to envisage an Egypt in which secular tensions are abated, the rule of law is encompassed. But I think it is going to take some time.

As I said earlier, I think we are at the early stages of a prolonged process, and it is going to require not only their patience, but also our patience as a friend of that country.

Ambassador ROSS. I agree with what Dan said. It takes time also to build what one might describe as a political culture of mutual adjustment. And they are going through a period right now where there is such a high degree of polarization that it is very difficult to adopt that kind of a mindset.

But they also have an interest in the future of their country and it seems to me that if you can build a process that is geared toward reconciliation, over time, this is something that can begin to emerge.

Dr. DUNNE. Senator, I think the issue of the role of religion in politics and public life is something that Egyptians are going to have to work through. In the Mubarak era, it was very, very tightly controlled, and Islamists could participate a bit politically, but in a very narrow way.

And then after Mubarak, the floodgates were wide open and they allowed religious slogans to be used in campaigns, and probably went too far to the other direction.

The Egyptians themselves will have to work out some sort of arrangement on this that everybody can live with and where there can be fair competition.

The CHAIRMAN. Well, thank you all for very in-depth analysis of this major issue and challenge for the United States. I think you have given us a lot of insight.

The record will remain open until the close of business on Friday.

And this hearing is adjourned.

[Whereupon, at 12:43 p.m., the hearing was adjourned.]